# Careers in Focus

# Careers in Focus

# SOCIAL WORK

## THIRD EDITION

Ferguson
*An imprint of Infobase Publishing*

Ferguson
An imprint of Infobase Publishing
132 West 31st Street
New York NY 10001

Library of Congress Cataloging-in-Publication Data

Careers in focus. Social work. — 3rd ed.
    p. cm.
Includes bibliographical references and index.
ISBN-13: 978-0-8160-8028-1 (hardcover : alk. paper)
ISBN-10: 0-8160-8028-3 (hardcover : alk. paper) 1. Social service—Vocational guidance—Juvenile literature. I. Ferguson Publishing. II. Title: Social work.
    HV10.5.C38 2010
    361.3023—dc22
                                    2010028516

Ferguson books are available at special discounts when purchased in bulk quantities for businesses, associations, institutions, or sales promotions. Please call our Special Sales Department in New York at (212) 967-8800 or (800) 322-8755.

You can find Ferguson on the World Wide Web at
http://www.infobasepublishing.com

Text design by David Strelecky
Composition by Mary Susan Ryan-Flynn
Cover printed by Art Print Company, Taylor, PA
Book printed and bound by Maple Press, York, PA
Date printed: December 2010
Printed in the United States of America

10 9 8 7 6 5 4 3 2 1

This book is printed on acid-free paper.

# Table of Contents

# Introduction

There are four categories of social services: individual and family services, residential care, job training and vocational rehabilitation services, and miscellaneous social services.

Individual and family services provide counseling and welfare services, including refugee, disaster, and temporary relief aid. This category includes the government offices that supply welfare assistance, rent supplements, and food stamps. It also includes agencies that provide adult day care and in-home services such as delivered meals, home health care, and chore services. Other services are child-oriented, such as big brother/big sister programs, child protective services, and adoption services. Counseling offered by crisis centers is also a part of this area of social work.

Residential care is round-the-clock personal and social care (excluding medical care) provided for the homeless, runaways, children, the elderly, alcohol and drug abusers, the mentally ill, the developmentally disabled, and others who are unable to care for themselves.

Job training and vocational rehabilitation services help the unemployed, disabled, and poorly educated learn new job skills or find jobs that fit their current skills.

Miscellaneous social services include groups that focus on social change and community improvement, such as advocacy groups, health and welfare councils, and antipoverty boards. They work at the administrative level to change social policy and raise and distribute funds to appropriate agencies.

The field of social work and social services is a dynamic one that can accommodate workers with a variety of skills and backgrounds. This book presents just a sampling of the many careers available in this growing field. In order to illustrate the different facets of social work, consider the example of a shelter. Shelters can operate only through the interaction of a variety of social service workers, from those who help clients budget for rent and groceries, to those who build houses for homeless families, to those who campaign for funds and write grant proposals.

Before a shelter can open, *policy makers* conduct research through surveys, interviews, and evaluations. They decide how to operate and finance the program. They answer questions such as: Is there a need for the shelter? Where is the best location? How many people will be served? How many people will be employed? Where can the money for operating costs come from? What services will be available? What impact will the shelter have on the neighborhood? *Fundraisers* and *grant writers* investigate the financial resources available for the project. Once funding is awarded and operating expenses can be met, the fund-monitoring staff keeps track of the money, a key aspect to an organization's survival.

Publicity is necessary for a shelter to inform the community of the services available and to convey the quality and success of the program. A *community outreach director* will work to educate the community about the problem of teen runaways. A *public relations specialist* may post notices about the shelter in areas frequented by runaways.

A shelter needs people to work directly with clients. *Counselors* and *therapists* conduct individual and group sessions. They also manage hotlines, providing counseling in crisis situations. *Social workers* or *psychologists* work with individuals to help them return to school or their homes, or to help prepare them for a foster home. These professionals also will evaluate client needs, and possibly recommend an extended program of service.

The staff at a shelter might include *tutors* to conduct individual lessons and study groups or *trainers* to help runaways get involved in school or community sports teams. *Employee-assistance personnel* might provide job counseling, interview skills, and special training.

According to the U.S. Department of Labor, opportunities in nongovernmental social services should be excellent through 2018, with 40 percent growth predicted in this area, as opposed to the 11 percent growth predicted for all industries combined. The large growth in this area is mainly due to the aging baby boom generation and growing elderly population, who will require many of the services that social workers provide in the coming years. In addition, services for the mentally ill, physically and developmentally disabled, and families in need will grow throughout the next decade, resulting in the need for more workers to provide these services. The area of home health care is one of the most promising in terms of available jobs. The number of home health care aides, for example, is expected to grow by 50 percent through 2018, which is much faster than the average growth predicted for all jobs.

Each article in *Careers in Focus: Social Work* discusses a particular occupation in detail. The articles appear in Ferguson's *Encyclopedia of Careers and Vocational Guidance*. Since the previous edition of this book, each article has been updated and revised with the latest information from the U.S. Department of Labor and other sources. Each article is broken down in the following manner.

The **Quick Facts** section provides a brief summary of the career, including recommended school subjects, personal skills, work environment, minimum educational requirements, salary ranges, certification or licensing requirements, and employment outlook. This section also provides acronyms and identification numbers for the following government classification indexes: the Dictionary of Occupational Titles (DOT), the Guide for Occupational Exploration (GOE), the National Occupational Classification (NOC) Index, and the Occupational Information Network (O*NET)-Standard Occupational Classification System (SOC) index. The DOT, GOE, and O*NET-SOC indexes have been created by the U.S. government; the NOC index is Canada's career classification system. Readers can use the identification numbers listed in the Quick Facts section to access further information about a career. Print editions of the DOT (*Dictionary of Occupational Titles.* Indianapolis, Ind.: JIST Works, 1991) and GOE (*Guide for Occupational Exploration.* Indianapolis, Ind.: JIST Works, 2001) are available at libraries. Electronic versions of the NOC (http://www5.hrsdc.gc.ca/NOC) and O*NET-SOC (http://online.onetcenter.org) are available on the Internet. When no DOT, GOE, NOC, or O*NET-SOC numbers are listed, this means that the U.S. Department of Labor or Human Resources and Skills Development Canada have not created a numerical designation for this career. In this instance, you will see the acronym "N/A," or not available.

The **Overview** section is a brief introductory description of the duties and responsibilities involved in this career. Oftentimes, a career may have a variety of job titles. When this is the case, alternative career titles are presented. Employment statistics are also provided, when available. The **History** section describes the history of the particular job as it relates to the overall development of its industry or field. The **Job** describes the primary and secondary duties of the job. **Requirements** discusses high school and postsecondary education and training requirements, any certification or licensing that is necessary, and other personal requirements for success in the job. **Exploring** offers suggestions on how to gain experience in or knowledge of the particular job before making a firm educational and financial commitment. The focus is on what can be done while still in high school (or in the early years of college) to gain a better understanding of the job. The **Employers** section gives an overview of typical places of employment for the job. **Starting Out** discusses the best ways to land that first job, be it through the college career services office, newspaper ads, Internet employment sites, or personal contact. The **Advancement** section describes what kind of career path to expect from the job and how to get there. **Earnings** lists salary ranges and describes the typical fringe benefits. The **Work Environment** section describes the typical surroundings and conditions of employment—whether indoors or outdoors, noisy or quiet, social or independent. Also discussed are typical hours worked, any seasonal fluctuations, and the stresses and strains of the job. The **Outlook** section summarizes the job in terms of the general economy and industry projections. For the most part, Outlook information is obtained from the U.S. Bureau of Labor Statistics and is supplemented by information gathered from professional associations. Job growth terms follow those used in the *Occupational Outlook Handbook*. Growth described as "much faster than the average" means an increase of 20 percent or more. Growth described as "faster than the average" means an increase of 14 to 19 percent. Growth described as "about as fast as the average" means an increase of 7 to 13 percent. Growth described as "more slowly than the average" means an increase of 3 to 6 percent. "Little or no change" means a decrease of 2 percent to an increase of 2 percent. "Decline" means a decrease of 3 percent or more. Each article ends with **For More Information,** which lists organizations that provide information on training, education, internships, scholarships, and job placement.

　　*Careers in Focus: Social Work* also includes photos, informative sidebars, and interviews with professionals in the field.

# Adult Day Care Coordinators

## OVERVIEW

*Adult day care coordinators*, also called *adult day services coordinators*, direct day service programs for adults who have physical or mental impairments or both. Clients of these programs are usually the elderly, although younger people with impairments, such as those recovering from strokes, may also participate in these programs. Coordinators oversee staff members who provide care, meals, and social activities to day care clients, and they serve as liaisons between their centers and their clients' families.

## HISTORY

Adult day care had its beginnings in the 1940s in psychiatric hospitals. It started as an effort to help patients who had been released from mental institutions. Over the next 20 years the focus gradually shifted from psychiatric care to other kinds of health maintenance. The landmark publication *Developing Day Care for Older People*, published by the National Council on Aging (NCOA) in 1972, provided technical assistance for establishing adult day care; by 1978 there were nearly 300 adult day care centers throughout the United States.

In the 1980s, the first congressional hearing was held on adult day care programs and the Economic Recovery Act was passed, allowing a tax credit to families with elderly members in day care. NCOA established voluntary standards.

## QUICK FACTS

**School Subjects**
Family and consumer science
Psychology
Sociology

**Personal Skills**
Helping/teaching
Leadership/management

**Work Environment**
Primarily indoors
Primarily one location

**Minimum Education Level**
Associate's degree

**Salary Range**
$18,000 to $55,000 to $94,000

**Certification or Licensing**
Required for certain positions

**Outlook**
Much faster than the average

**DOT**
354

**GOE**
N/A

**NOC**
N/A

**O*NET-SOC**
N/A

According to the National Adult Day Services Association, more than 4,600 adult day centers are currently operating in the United States. Nearly 78 percent operate on a nonprofit or public basis, and many are affiliated with larger organizations such as home care, skilled nursing facilities, medical centers, or multipurpose senior organizations.

## THE JOB

Adult day care coordinators direct adult day care centers. Although specific duties vary depending on the size of the center and the services it offers, the general responsibility of coordinators is to ensure that their centers provide the necessary care for clients. Such care may include attention to personal hygiene and providing meals, medications, therapies, and social activities.

Although coordinators working in small day care centers may actually perform some services for clients, this is not the norm. Instead, coordinators usually oversee various staff members who provide the caregiving. A large center, for example, might have a nurse, physical therapist, social worker, cook, and several aides. Coordinators are responsible for staff hiring, training, and scheduling. They may meet with staff members either one-on-one or in group sessions to review and discuss plans for the clients.

Overseeing meal planning and preparation is also the responsibility of the adult day services coordinator. In most centers, clients are given a midday meal and usually juices and snacks in the morning and afternoon. Coordinators work with a cook or dietitian to develop well-rounded menus that take into account the nutritional needs of the clients, including any particular restrictions such as diabetic or low-sodium diets. The coordinator may also oversee purchasing and taking inventory of the center's food supply.

The coordinator schedules daily and weekly activities for the day care clients. Depending on the particular needs and abilities of the clients, a recreational schedule might include crafts, games, exercises, reading time, or movies. In some centers, clients are taken on outings to shopping centers, parks, or restaurants. The coordinator plans such outings, arranging for transportation and any reservations or special accommodations that may be necessary. Finally, the coordinator also organizes parties for special events, such as holidays and birthdays.

Finding new activities and visitors for the center is also part of the job. Coordinators might recruit volunteers to teach crafts or music to the clients. Often, religious or civic groups come to such facilities to visit with clients. Some such groups institute buddy programs, in which each group member pairs with a day care client to develop an ongoing relationship. The day care coordinator must authorize and monitor any group visits, activities, or programs.

In addition to planning and overseeing the activities of the center and its clients, the adult day care coordinator also works closely with client family members to make sure that each individual is receiving care that best fits his or her needs. This relationship with the client's family usually begins before the client is placed in the day care center.

When a family is considering placing an elderly relative in day care, they often have many questions about the center and its activities. The coordinator meets with family members to show them the center and explain to them how it is run. The coordinator also gathers information about the potential client, including names and phone numbers of doctors and people to contact in case of emergency, lists of medications taken with instructions on when and how they should be administered, and information on allergies, food choices, and daily habits and routines.

After the client is placed in the center, the coordinator may meet periodically with the client's family to update them on how the client is responding to the day care setting. If necessary, the coordinator may advise the family about social services, such as home health care, and refer them to other providers.

Adult day care coordinators may have other duties, depending on the center and how it is owned and operated. For example, they may be responsible for developing and adhering to a budget for the center. In centers licensed or certified by the state, coordinators may ensure

## Facts About Social Assistance, 2008

- About 1.6 million nongovernment social assistance workers were employed in the United States.

- Approximately 71 percent of these workers were employed in individual and family services, with the remaining workers employed in vocational rehabilitation services (20.3 percent) and emergency and other relief services (8.7 percent).

- Employment in the field of social assistance is expected to grow by 40 percent from 2008 to 2018—much faster than the average for all industries.

Source: U.S. Department of Labor

that their centers remain in compliance with the regulations and necessary documentation. They may also be responsible for general bookkeeping, bill payment, and office management.

In addition to supervising centers, coordinators may also promote and advertise to the community. They may help with fund-raising, prepare press releases, and speak to various service clubs.

# REQUIREMENTS

## High School
While you are in high school, you should take classes that prepare you for postsecondary training. These include mathematics, business, family and consumer science classes as well as science classes, such as biology. To improve your understanding of people, take history, psychology, and sociology classes. Because communication is an important skill, English and speech classes are also good choices.

## Postsecondary Training
Because this is a relatively new and growing field, there are no national standards to follow for becoming an adult day care coordinator. Some people have learned their skills on the job; others have taken courses in home nursing or health care; still others have completed associate's or bachelor's degrees in areas such as health and human services. As the need for and popularity of day care services continue to grow, more employers will begin to expect coordinators to have at least some formal education.

Many employers prefer to hire candidates who meet the standards set by the National Adult Day Services Association (NADSA). In order to meet these standards, a coordinator must have a bachelor's degree in health or social services or a related field, with one year's supervisory experience in a social or health services setting. In preparation for such a career, a college student might choose occupational, recreational, or rehabilitation therapy, or social work or human development. An increasingly popular major for potential adult day care coordinators is gerontology, or geriatrics.

The Association for Gerontology in Higher Education publishes the *Directory of Educational Programs in Gerontology and Geriatrics,* which contains information on programs available from the associate's to the post-doctorate level. Although specific courses vary from school to school, most programs consist of classes in social gerontology, biology and physiology of aging, psychology of aging, and sociology of aging. In addition to these four core classes, most programs offer elective courses in such areas as social policy, community services, nutrition and exercise, diversity in aging, health issues, death and dying, and ethics and life extension.

A practicum or field placement is also a part of most gerontology programs. This allows students to obtain experience working with both well-functioning elderly people and those with age-related disabilities.

### Certification or Licensing

The National Certification Council for Activity Professionals offers certification to activity directors. See the end of the article for contact information.

Regulations can vary by state. In some states, for example, the agency that a coordinator works for must be licensed or certified by the state health department. Any adult day care center that receives payment from Medicare or from other government programs must be certified by the state department of health. In these cases, licensing requirements may include requirements for coordinators and other staff members. The trend is toward stricter standards.

### Other Requirements

Regardless of what level of education a prospective coordinator has, there are certain personal characteristics that are necessary for success in this field. Compassion and an affinity for the elderly and disabled are vital, as are patience and the desire to help others. You should also be organized and able to manage other workers effectively. Communication skills are very important since you will be working with staff, clients, regulatory agencies, and clients' families.

## EXPLORING

There are several ways you can learn more about the career of adult day care coordinator. The first and easiest way is to check your local library for books or articles on aging in order to learn more about the elderly, their issues, and the services available to them. Resources are also available on the Internet. Next, visit a nursing home or adult day care center in order to experience firsthand what it is like to spend time with and interact with elderly people. Arrange to talk with staff members and the center's coordinator to find out what their day-to-day jobs are like. Your high school counselor may also be able to arrange for a coordinator to give a career talk at your school. Finally, get a volunteer position or part-time job in such a facility. This will allow you to gauge your aptitude for a career in adult day care work.

## EMPLOYERS

Adult day care coordinators work at adult day care centers. These may be small or large. It is estimated that there are more than 4,600 adult day care centers currently operating in the United States. Most of them are operated on a nonprofit or public basis, and many are affiliated with large organizations such as nursing homes, hospitals, or multipurpose senior organizations. Standards and work environments vary.

## STARTING OUT

In looking for a position as an adult day care coordinator, candidates should first locate and contact all such programs in the area. Checking the local Yellow Pages under Nursing Homes, Residential Care Facilities, Aging Services, or Senior Citizens Services should provide a list of leads. The job seeker might either send a resume and cover letter or call these potential employers directly. Prospective coordinators should also watch for job openings listed in area newspapers and on organizations' Web sites.

Another means of finding job leads is to become affiliated with a professional association, such as the American Geriatrics Society, the American Association of Homes and Services for the Aging, the Gerontological Society of America, or the National Council on Aging. Many such organizations have monthly or quarterly newsletters that list job opportunities. Some may even have job banks or referral services.

Job seekers who have received associate's or bachelor's degrees should also check with the career services offices at their colleges or universities.

## ADVANCEMENT

Because the field of aging-related services continues to grow, the potential for advancement for adult day care coordinators is good. Some coordinators advance by transferring to a larger center that pays better wages. Others eventually start their own centers. Still others advance by moving into management positions in other, similar social service organizations, such as nursing homes, hospices, or government agencies on aging.

An adult day care coordinator might choose to return to school and complete a higher degree, often a master's degree in social work. For those who choose this option, there are many career opportunities in the field of social services. Social workers, for example, work with individuals and families dealing with AIDS, cancer, or other debilitating illnesses. They also work for agencies offering various types of counseling, rehabilitation, or crisis intervention.

## EARNINGS

Starting salaries for this position depend partly on the experience and education of the coordinator and partly upon the size and location of the day care center. Larger centers located in metropolitan areas tend to offer the highest wages.

According to the Association for Gerontology in Higher Education, beginning salaries range from $18,000 to $31,000 for persons with a bachelor's degree and little experience. Generally, coordinators who do not have a bachelor's degree can expect to earn somewhat less. Experienced coordinators with a bachelor's degree employed in large, well-funded centers may earn from $32,000 to $94,000 annually, with a median salary of $55,000.

In addition to salary, some coordinators are also offered a benefits package, which typically includes health insurance, paid vacation and sick days, and a retirement plan.

## WORK ENVIRONMENT

Most adult day care centers have a schedule that corresponds to standard business hours. Most coordinators work a 40-hour week, Monday through Friday, with weekends off.

The coordinator's work environment will vary depending on the size and type of center he or she supervises. Some centers are fairly institutional, resembling children's day care centers or nursing homes. Others have a more residential feel, being carpeted and furnished like a private home. Regardless of the furnishings, the center is typically clean, well lit, and equipped with ramps, rails, and other devices that ensure the safety of clients.

Part of the coordinator's day may be spent in the center's common areas with clients and staff. He or she may also spend time working in an on-site office. If the staff members take clients on outings, the coordinator may accompany them.

Coordinators are on their feet much of the time, ensuring that meals and activities run smoothly and helping staff members when necessary. Attire for the job varies from center to center, ranging from very casual to standard office wear. Most coordinators, however, wear clothing that is comfortable and allows them freedom of movement.

Regardless of the size of the center, coordinators spend the majority of their time working with people, both staff members and day care clients. Working with clients is often very trying. Many of them may have had a stroke or have Alzheimer's disease, and they may be confused, uncooperative, or even hostile. The job may also be emotionally taxing for the coordinator who becomes attached to his or her clients. Most adults who use a day care center are elderly or permanently disabled; for this reason, day care staff must frequently deal with the decline and eventual death of their clients.

## OUTLOOK

The outlook for all human services workers, and adult day care coordinators in particular, is expected to be excellent through 2018, growing at a rate that is much faster than the average. The main reason for this is that the senior citizen population is growing rapidly. According to a study conducted by the U.S. Census Bureau, by 2050 there will be 82 million older persons in the United States, which is more than twice the number that existed in 1999. Coupled with this growing elderly population will be a decreasing number of caregivers because of increased divorce rates, smaller families, delayed child-bearing trends, and more men and women in the workforce. Given these projections, adult day care will be used more frequently as a cost-efficient and preferable alternative to nursing homes.

## FOR MORE INFORMATION

*For information on careers and aging and services for the elderly, contact*
American Association of Homes and Services for the Aging
2519 Connecticut Avenue, NW
Washington, DC 20008-1520
Tel: 202-783-2242
E-mail: info@aahsa.org
http://www.aahsa.org

*AGHE, a section of the Gerontological Society of America, promotes education in the field of aging and offers a directory of gerontology and geriatrics programs.*
Association for Gerontology in Higher Education (AGHE)
1220 L Street, NW, Suite 901
Washington, DC 20005-4018
Tel: 202-289-9806
http://www.aghe.org

*For career information and student resources, contact*
Gerontological Society of America
1220 L Street, NW, Suite 901
Washington, DC 20005-4001
Tel: 202-842-1275
http://www.geron.org

*For information on the history of adult day service and day service facts, contact*
National Adult Day Services Association
85 South Washington Street
Seattle, WA 98104-3405
Tel: 877-745-1440
E-mail: info@nadsa.org
http://www.nadsa.org

*This organization can provide information on services, including adult day care, available across the country.*
National Association of Area Agencies on Aging
1730 Rhode Island Avenue, NW, Suite 1200
Washington, DC 20036-3109
Tel: 202-872-0888
http://www.n4a.org

*For information on certification, contact*
National Certification Council for Activity Professionals
PO Box 62589
Virginia Beach, VA 23466-2589
Tel: 757-552-0653
E-mail: info@nccap.org
http://www.nccap.org

*To learn about developments and current issues in the aging field, visit the following Web site:*
National Council on Aging
1901 L Street, NW, 4th Floor
Washington, DC 20036-3540
Tel: 202-479-1200
http://www.ncoa.org

# Alcohol and Drug Abuse Counselors

## QUICK FACTS

**School Subjects**
Health
Psychology
Sociology

**Personal Skills**
Communication/ideas
Helping/teaching

**Work Environment**
Primarily indoors
Primarily one location

**Minimum Education Level**
Bachelor's degree

**Salary Range**
$24,580 to $37,700 to
$60,060+

**Certification or Licensing**
Recommended (certification)
Required by certain states
(licensing)

**Outlook**
Much faster than the average

**DOT**
045

**GOE**
12.02.02

**NOC**
N/A

**O*NET-SOC**
21-1011.00

## OVERVIEW

*Alcohol and drug abuse counselors* (sometimes called *substance abuse counselors*) work with people who abuse or are addicted to drugs or alcohol. Through individual and group counseling sessions, they help their clients understand and change their destructive substance abuse behaviors. There are about 86,100 substance abuse and behavioral disorder counselors in the United States.

## HISTORY

Throughout history people have used drugs for a variety of purposes—for healing, for religious ceremonies, to alter consciousness for self-understanding, to loosen inhibitions and have fun, or to dull the senses against emotional or physical pain. Alcohol and other substances were used in ancient Egypt, Greece, and India as offerings to spiritual beings, as well as to reach a higher consciousness. Many religions today, from Tibetan Buddhism and traditional Native American religions to Roman Catholicism, use alcohol and other consciousness-altering substances in traditional ceremonies.

Throughout the ages people have abused drugs and alcohol too. No matter what the purpose for the initial drug use, it becomes for some people an obsession, and then an addiction. The history of treatment for substance abuse is much shorter. In the 1800s, alcoholics and morphine addicts were placed in asylums. Treatments sometimes included miracle medicines that were sup-

14

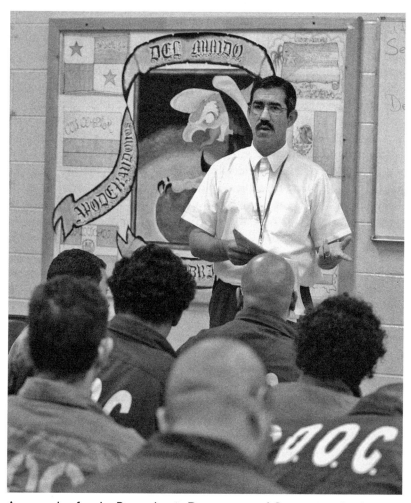

A counselor for the Pennsylvania Department of Corrections leads a session to treat Spanish-speaking inmates with drug and alcohol abuse problems. *(Carolyn Kaster, AP Photo)*

posed to be quick "cures" for addicts. In the early 1900s, doctors used electroshock therapies and psychosurgery to treat alcoholics.

In 1935, the Alcoholics Anonymous (AA) program was started by two men known as Bill and Dr. Bob. They helped each other achieve sobriety and continued to help others. This system of alcoholics helping other alcoholics grew into the AA movement, which is still strong today. AA's 12-step program has been adapted and used effectively to treat addictions of all kinds.

Today alcohol and a huge variety of dangerous drugs are readily available—marijuana, cocaine, LSD, heroin, inhalants, amphetamines, barbiturates, club drugs, and more. Fortunately, treatment programs are also readily available for those who want them. Outpatient methadone programs give heroin addicts the medication methadone to reduce cravings for heroin and block its effects. Patients are also counseled, given vocational guidance and training, and taught how to find support services. Long-term residential programs last for several months to a year. Patients live in a drug-free environment with fellow recovering addicts and counselors. Outpatient drug-free programs use such therapies as problem-solving groups, insight-oriented psychotherapy, cognitive-behavioral therapy, and 12-step programs. Short-term inpatient programs focus on stabilizing the patient, abstinence, and lifestyle changes.

## THE JOB

The main goal of alcohol and drug abuse counselors is to help patients stop their destructive behaviors. Counselors may also work with the families of clients to give them support and guidance in dealing with the problem.

Counselors begin by trying to learn about a patient's general background and history of drug or alcohol use. They may review patient records, including police reports, employment records, medical records, or reports from other counselors.

Counselors also interview the patient to determine the nature and extent of substance abuse. During an interview, the counselor asks questions about what types of substances the patient uses, how often, and for how long. The counselor may also ask patients about previous attempts to stop using the substance and about how the problem has affected their lives in various respects.

Using the information they obtain from the patient and their knowledge of substance abuse patterns, counselors formulate a program for treatment and rehabilitation. A substantial part of the rehabilitation process involves individual, group, or family counseling sessions. During individual sessions, counselors do a great deal of listening, perhaps asking appropriate questions to guide patients to insights about themselves. In group therapy sessions, counselors supervise groups of several patients, helping move their discussion in positive ways. In counseling sessions, counselors also teach patients methods of overcoming their dependencies. For example, they might help a patient develop a series of goals for behavioral change.

Counselors monitor and assess the progress of their patients. In most cases, counselors deal with several different patients in various stages of recovery—some may need help breaking the pattern of substance abuse; some may already have stopped using, but still need support; others may be recovered users who have suffered a relapse. Counselors maintain ongoing relationships with patients to help them adapt to the different recovery stages.

Working with families is another aspect of many alcohol and drug abuse counselors' jobs. They may ask a patient's family for insight into the patient's behavior. They may also teach the patient's family members how to deal with and support the patient through the recovery process.

Counselors may work with other health professionals and social agencies, including physicians, psychiatrists, psychologists, employment services, and court systems. In some cases, the counselor, with the patient's permission, may serve as a spokesperson for the patient, working with corrections officers, social workers, or employers. In other cases, a patient's needs might exceed the counselor's abilities; when this is the case, the counselor refers the patient to an appropriate medical expert, agency, or social program.

There is a substantial amount of paperwork involved in counseling alcohol and drug abusers. Detailed records must be kept on patients in order to follow their progress. For example, a report must be written after each counseling session. Counselors who work in residential treatment settings are required to participate in regular staff meetings to develop treatment plans and review patient progress. They may also meet periodically with family members or social service agency representatives to discuss patient progress and needs.

In some cases, alcohol and drug abuse counselors specialize in working with certain groups of people. Some work only with children or teenagers; others work with businesses to counsel employees who may have problems related to drugs and alcohol. In still other cases, counselors specialize in treating people who are addicted to specific drugs, such as cocaine, heroin, or alcohol. Counselors may need special training in order to work with specific groups.

# REQUIREMENTS
## High School
High school students who are considering a career in alcohol and drug abuse counseling should choose a curriculum that meets the requirements of the college or university they hope to attend. Typically, four years of English, history, mathematics, a foreign language, and social sciences are necessary. In addition, psychology, sociology, physiology, biology, and anatomy provide a good academic background for potential counselors.

The educational requirements for alcohol and drug abuse counselors vary greatly by state and employer. A high school education may be the minimum requirement for employers who provide on-the-job training, which ranges from six weeks to two years. These jobs, however, are becoming increasingly rare as more states are leaning toward stricter requirements for counselors.

## Postsecondary Training
Most substance abuse counselors, however, have a bachelor's degree in counseling, psychology, health sociology, or social work. Many two- and four-year colleges now offer specific courses for students training to be substance abuse counselors.

Many counselors have a master's degree in counseling with a specialization in substance abuse counseling. A master's degree is required to become licensed or certified as a counselor. Accredited graduate programs in substance abuse counseling are composed of a supervised internship as well as regular classwork.

## Certification or Licensing
The NAADAC, the Association for Addiction Professionals offers several professional designations, including national certified addiction counselor, master addiction counselor, tobacco addiction specialist credential, substance abuse professional qualification, certificate in spiritual caregiving to help addicted persons and families, conflict resolution in recovery certificate, and adolescent specialist endorsement. Additionally, the National Board for Certified Counselors offers the master addiction counselor designation to counselors who hold the national certified counselor designation and meet educational and professional experience requirements.

Currently, 49 states (not California) and the District of Columbia have credentialing laws for alcohol and drug abuse counselors. These laws typically require that counselors have a minimum of a master's degree and two to three years of postacademic supervised counseling experience. Candidates must also have passed a written test.

## Other Requirements
In order to be successful in this job, you should enjoy working with people. You must have compassion, good communication and listening skills, and a desire to help others. You should also be emotionally stable and able to deal with the frustrations and failures that are often a part of the job.

# EXPLORING

Students interested in this career can find a great deal of information on substance abuse and substance abuse counseling at any local library or on the Internet. In addition, by contacting a local hospital, mental health clinic, or treatment center, it might be possible to talk with a counselor about the details of his or her job.

Volunteer work or a part-time job at a residential facility such as a hospital or treatment center is another good way of gaining experience and exploring an aptitude for counseling work. Finally, the professional and government organizations listed at the end of this article can provide information on alcohol and drug abuse counseling.

# EMPLOYERS

Approximately 86,100 substance abuse and behavioral disorder counselors are employed in the United States. Counselors are hired by hospitals, private and public treatment centers, government agencies, prisons, public school systems, colleges and universities, health maintenance organizations (HMOs), crisis centers, and mental health centers. More and more frequently, large companies are hiring alcohol and drug abuse counselors as well, to deal with employee substance abuse problems.

# STARTING OUT

Counselors who have completed a two- or four-year college degree might start a job search by checking with the career services office of their college or university. Those who plan to look for a position without first attending college might want to start by getting an entry-level or volunteer position in a treatment center or related agency. In this way, they can obtain practical experience and also make connections that might lead to full-time employment as a counselor.

Job seekers should also watch the classified advertisements in local newspapers. Job openings for counselors are often listed under "Alcohol and Drug Counselor," "Substance Abuse Counselor," or "Mental Health Counselor." Finally, one might consider applying directly to the personnel department of various facilities and agencies that treat alcohol and drug abusers.

# ADVANCEMENT

Counselors in this field often advance initially by taking on more responsibilities and earning a higher wage. They may also better themselves by taking a similar position in a more prestigious facility, such as an upscale private treatment center.

As they obtain more experience and perhaps more education, counselors sometimes move into supervisory or administrative positions. They might become directors of substance abuse programs in mental health facilities or executive directors of agencies or clinics.

Career options are more diverse for those counselors who continue their education. They may move into research, consulting, or teaching at the college level.

## EARNINGS

Salaries of alcohol and drug abuse counselors depend on education level, amount of experience, and place of employment. Generally, the more education and experience a counselor has, the higher his or her earnings will be. Counselors who work in private treatment centers also tend to earn more than their public sector counterparts.

Alcohol and drug abuse counselors earned a median annual salary of $37,700 in 2009, according to the U.S. Department of Labor. The lowest paid 10 percent earned less than $24,580. The highest paid 10 percent earned $60,060 or more. Directors of treatment programs or centers could earn considerably more than the national median salary. Almost all treatment centers provide employee benefits to their full-time counselors. Benefits usually include paid vacations and sick days, insurance, and pension plans.

## WORK ENVIRONMENT

The hours that an alcohol and drug abuse counselor works depend upon where he or she is employed. Many residential treatment facilities and mental health centers—and all crisis centers—have counselors on duty during evening and weekend hours. Other employers, such as government agencies and universities, are likely to have more conventional working hours.

Work settings for counselors also vary by employer. Counselors may work in private offices, in the rooms or homes of patients, in classrooms, or in meeting rooms. In some cases, they conduct support group sessions in churches, community centers, or schools. For the most part, however, counselors work at the same work site or sites on a daily basis.

The bulk of a counselor's day is spent dealing with various people—patients, families, social workers, and health care professionals.

There may be very little time during a workday for quiet reflection or organization.

Working with alcohol and drug abusers can be emotionally draining. Overcoming addiction is a very hard battle, and patients respond to it in various ways. They may be resentful, angry, discouraged, or profoundly depressed. They may talk candidly with their counselors about tragic and upsetting events in their lives. Counselors spend much of their time listening to and dealing with very strong, usually negative, emotions.

This work can also be discouraging, due to a high failure rate. Many alcoholics and drug addicts do not respond to treatment and return immediately to their addictions. Even after months and sometimes years of recovery, many substance abusers suffer relapses. The counselor must learn to cope with the frustration of having his or her patients fail, perhaps repeatedly.

There is a very positive side to drug and alcohol abuse counseling, however. When it is successful, counselors have the satisfaction of knowing that they had a positive effect on someone's life. They have the reward of seeing some patients return to happy family lives and productive careers.

## OUTLOOK

Employment of alcohol and drug abuse counselors is projected to grow much faster than the average for all occupations through 2018, according to the U.S. Department of Labor. There are nearly 18 million alcoholics in the United States and an equal, if not greater, number of drug abusers. Because no successful method to significantly reduce drug and alcohol abuse has emerged, these numbers are not likely to decrease. Overall population growth will also lead to a need for more substance abuse counselors. Finally, many states are shifting away from criminalizing drug use, seeing it as a mental-health problem that should be treated through the medical system, not the criminal-justice system.

Another reason for the expected growth in counselors' jobs is that an increasing number of employers are offering employee assistance programs that provide counseling services for mental health and alcohol and drug abuse.

Finally, many job openings will arise as a result of job turnover. Because of the stress levels and the emotional demands involved in this career, there is a high burnout rate. As alcohol and drug abuse counselors leave the field, new counselors are needed to replace them.

# FOR MORE INFORMATION

*For more information on substance abuse and counseling careers, contact*
American Counseling Association
5999 Stevenson Avenue
Alexandria, VA 22304-3304
Tel: 800-347-6647
http://www.counseling.org

*For information on certification, contact*
NAADAC, The Association for Addiction Professionals
1001 North Fairfax Street, Suite 201
Alexandria, VA 22314-1587
Tel: 800-548-0497
E-mail: naadac@naadac.org
http://www.naadac.org

*For information on certification, contact*
National Board for Certified Counselors
3 Terrace Way
Greensboro, NC 27403-3660
Tel: 336-547-0607
E-mail: nbcc@nbcc.org
http://www.nbcc.org

*For additional information, check out the following Web site run by the Substance Abuse and Mental Health Services Administration and the U.S. Department of Health and Human Services:*
National Clearinghouse for Alcohol and Drug Information
http://ncadi.samhsa.gov

*For more information about alcohol and substance abuse, contact the following organizations:*
National Institute on Alcohol Abuse and Alcoholism
National Institutes of Health
5635 Fishers Lane, MSC 9304
Bethesda, MD 20892-9304
Tel: 301-443-3860
http://www.niaaa.nih.gov

National Institute on Drug Abuse
National Institutes of Health

6001 Executive Boulevard, Room 5213
Bethesda, MD 20892-9561
Tel: 301-443-1124
E-mail: information@nida.nih.gov
http://www.nida.nih.gov

# Career and Employment Counselors and Technicians

## OVERVIEW

*Career and employment counselors,* who are also known as *vocational counselors,* provide advice to individuals or groups about occupations, careers, career decision making, career planning, and other career development-related questions or conflicts. *Career guidance technicians* collect pertinent information to support both the counselor and applicant during the job search. Approximately 275,800 educational, vocational, and school counselors are employed in the United States.

## HISTORY

The first funded employment office in the United States was established in San Francisco in 1886. However, it was not until the turn of the century that public interest in improving educational conditions began to develop. The Civic Service House in Boston began the United States' first program of vocational guidance, and the Vocational Bureau was established in 1908 to help young people choose, train, and enter appropriate careers.

The idea of vocational counseling became so appealing that by 1910 a national conference on vocational

24

guidance was held in Boston. The federal government gave support to vocational counseling by initiating a program to assist veterans of World War I in readjusting to civilian life. Agencies such as the Civilian Conservation Corps and the National Youth Administration made attempts at vocational counseling during the Depression years.

**QUICK FACTS**

*(continued)*

**GOE**
12.03.01

**NOC**
4143, 4213

**O*NET-SOC**
21-1012.00, 21-1093.00

On June 6, 1933, the Wagner-Peyser Act established the United States Employment Service. States came into the service one by one, with each state developing its own plan under the prescribed limits of the act. By the end of World War II, the Veterans Administration was counseling more than 50,000 veterans each month. Other state and federal government agencies now involved with vocational guidance services include the Bureau of Indian Affairs, the Bureau of Apprenticeship and Training, and the Department of Education. In 1980, the National Career Development Association (NCDA), founded in 1913, established a committee for the pre-service and in-service training of vocational guidance personnel. The NCDA established a national credentialing process in 1984.

The profession of employment counseling has become important to the welfare of society as well as to the individuals within it. Each year millions of people need help in acquiring the kinds of information that make it possible for them to take advantage of today's career opportunities.

## THE JOB

Certified career counselors help people make decisions and plan life and career directions. They tailor strategies and techniques to the specific needs of the person seeking help. Counselors conduct individual and group counseling sessions to help identify life and career goals. They administer and interpret tests and inventories to assess abilities and interests and identify career options. They may use career planning and occupational information to help individuals better understand the work world. They assist in developing individualized career plans, teach job-hunting strategies and skills, and help develop resumes. Sometimes this involves resolving personal conflicts on the job. They also provide support for people experiencing job stress, job loss, and career transition.

A good counselor knows the working world and how to obtain detailed information about specific jobs. To assist with career decisions, counselors must know about the availability of jobs, the probable future of certain jobs, the education or training necessary to enter them, the kinds of salary or other benefits that certain jobs offer, the conditions that certain jobs impose on employees (night work, travel, work outdoors), and the satisfaction that certain jobs provide their employees. Career counselors work in both private and public settings and are certified by the National Board for Certified Counselors (NBCC).

*College career planning counselors* and *college placement counselors* work exclusively with the students of their universities or colleges. They are sometimes known as *college career services counselors*. They may specialize in some specific area appropriate to the students and graduates of the school, such as law and education, as well as in part-time and summer work, internships, and field placements. In a liberal arts college, the students may need more assistance in identifying an appropriate career. To do this, the counselor administers interest and aptitude tests and interviews students to determine their career goals. Counselors also give assistance in preparing the actual job search by helping the applicant to write resumes and letters of application, as well as by practicing interview skills through role-playing and other techniques. They also provide information on business procedures and personnel requirements in the applicant's chosen field. University-based counselors will set up online accounts on career Web sites for students, giving them access to information regarding potential employers. The counselor may work with currently enrolled students who are seeking internships and other work programs while still at school. Alumni who wish to make a career change also seek the services of the career counseling and services office at their former schools.

College placement counselors gather job information from prospective employers and make the information available to interested students and alumni. Just as counselors try to find applicants for particular job listings, they also must seek out jobs for specific applicants. To do this, they will contact potential employers to encourage them to consider a qualified individual. College placement counselors are responsible for the arrangements and details of on-campus interviews by large corporations. They also maintain an up-to-date library of guidance material and recruitment literature, as well as Web and other electronic resources.

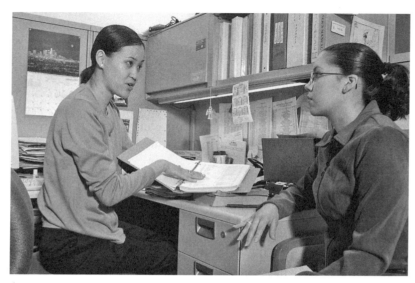

A career counselor talks to a job-seeker who is looking for secretarial work. (*Bob Daemmrich, The Image Works*)

Some career planning and placement counselors work with secondary school authorities, advising them on the needs of local industries and specific preparation requirements for both employment and further education. In two-year colleges the counselor may participate in the planning of course content, and in some smaller schools the counselor may be required to teach as well.

*Vocational-rehabilitation counselors* work with disabled individuals to help the counselees understand what skills they have to offer to an employer.

The principal duty of career guidance technicians is to help order, catalog, and file materials relating to job opportunities, careers, technical schools, scholarships, careers in the armed forces, and other programs. Guidance technicians also help students and teachers find materials relating to a student's interests and aptitudes. These various materials may be in the form of print and electronic books, pamphlets, magazine articles, videos, podcasts, computer software, or other media.

Often, career guidance technicians help students take and score self-administered tests that determine their aptitude and interest in different careers or job-related activities. If the career guidance center has audiovisual equipment, such as DVD players or film or slide projectors, career guidance technicians are usually responsible for the equipment.

# REQUIREMENTS

## High School

In order to work in the career and employment counseling field, you must have at least a high school diploma. For most jobs in the field, however, higher education is required. In high school, in addition to studying a core curriculum, with courses in English, history, mathematics, and biology, you should take courses in psychology and sociology. You will also find it helpful to take business and computer science classes.

## Postsecondary Training

In some states, the minimum educational requirement in career and vocational counseling is a graduate degree in counseling or a related field from a regionally accredited higher education institution, and a completed supervised counseling experience, which includes career counseling. A growing number of institutions offer post-master's degrees with training in career development and career counseling. Such programs are highly recommended if you wish to specialize in vocational and career counseling. These programs are frequently called advanced graduate specialist programs or certificates of advanced study programs.

For a career as a college career and employment counselor, the minimum educational requirement is commonly a master's degree in guidance and counseling, education, college student personnel work, behavioral science, or a related field. Graduate work includes courses in vocational and aptitude testing, counseling techniques, personnel management and occupational research, industrial relations, and group dynamics and organizational behavior.

As in any profession, there is usually an initial period of training for newly hired counselors and counselor trainees. Some of the skills you will need as an employment counselor, such as testing-procedures skills and interviewing skills, can be acquired only through on-the-job training.

When hiring a career guidance technician, most employers look for applicants who have completed two years of training beyond high school, usually at a junior, community, or technical college. These two-year programs, which usually lead to an associate's degree, may combine classroom instruction with practical or sometimes even on-the-job experience.

## Certification or Licensing

The NBCC offers the national certified counselor (NCC) designation as well as the national certified school counselor (NCSC) designation. In order to apply for the NCC, you must have earned a master's degree with a major study in counseling and you must pass the National Counselor Examination. NCCs are certified for a period of five years. In order to be recertified, they must complete 100 contact clock hours of continuing education or pass the examination again. In order to receive the NCSC credential, you must complete the above requirements, plus gain field experience in school counseling as a graduate student and then complete three years of post-graduate supervised school counseling. Nearly all states require some type of credentialing or certification for counselors, and all states require those who work in school settings to be certified.

### Other Requirements
In order to succeed as a career counselor, you must have a good background in education, training, employment trends, the current labor market, and career resources. You should be able to provide your clients with information about job tasks, functions, salaries, requirements, and the future outlook of broad occupational fields. Knowledge of testing techniques and measures of aptitude, achievement, interests, values, and personality is required. The ability to evaluate job performance and individual effectiveness is helpful. You must also have management and administrative skills. Career guidance technicians should have good organizational and communication skills and be able to follow instructions.

## EXPLORING
Summer work in an employment agency is a good way to explore the field of employment counseling. Interviewing the director of a public or private agency might give you a better understanding of what the work involves and the qualifications such an organization requires of its counselors.

If you enjoy working with others, you will find helpful experiences working in the dean's or counselor's office. Many schools offer opportunities in peer tutoring, both in academics and in career guidance duties. (If your school does not have such a program in place, consider putting together a proposal to institute one. Your counselor should be able to help you with this.) Your own experience in seeking summer and part-time work is also valuable in learning what job seekers must confront in business or industry. You could write a feature story for your school newspaper on your and others' experiences in the working world.

If you are interested in becoming a career counselor, you should seek out professional career counselors and discuss the field with them. Most people are happy to talk about what they do.

While in high school, consider working part time or as a volunteer in a library. Such work can provide you with some of the basic skills for learning about information resources, cataloging, and filing. In addition, assisting schools or clubs with any media presentations, such as video or PowerPoint presentations, will help you become familiar with the equipment and software used by counselors. You may also find it helpful to read publications relating to this field, such as *The National Certified Counselor* newsletter (http://www.nbcc.org/newsletter).

## EMPLOYERS

There are approximately 275,800 educational, vocational, and school counselors employed in the United States. Career and employment counselors work in counseling offices and career centers of high schools, colleges, and universities. They are also employed by state, federal, and other bureaus of employment, and by social service agencies.

## STARTING OUT

Journals specializing in information for career counselors frequently have job listings or information on job hotlines and services. School career services offices also are a good source of information, both because of their standard practice of listing job openings from participating firms and because schools are a likely source of jobs for you as a career counselor. Placement officers will be aware of which schools are looking for applicants.

To enter the field of college career planning and placement, you might consider working for your alma mater as an assistant in the career services office. Other occupational areas that provide an excellent background for college placement work include teaching, business, public relations, previous placement training, positions in employment agencies, and experience in psychological counseling.

Career guidance technicians should receive some form of career placement from schools offering training in that area. Newspapers may list entry-level jobs. One of the best methods, however, is to contact libraries and education centers directly to inquire about their needs for assistance in developing or staffing their career guidance centers.

# ADVANCEMENT

Employment counselors in federal or state employment services or in other vocational counseling agencies are usually considered trainees for the first six months of their employment. During this time, they learn the specific skills that will be expected of them during their careers with these agencies. The first year of a new counselor's employment is probationary.

Positions of further responsibility include supervisory or administrative work, which may be attained by counselors after several years of experience on the job. Advancement to administrative positions often means giving up the actual counseling work, which is not an advantage to those who enjoy working with people in need of counseling.

Opportunity for advancement for college counselors—to assistant and associate placement director, director of student personnel services, or similar administrative positions—depends largely on the type of college or university and the size of the staff. In general, a doctorate is preferred and may be necessary for advancement.

With additional education, career guidance technicians can advance to become career and employment counselors.

# EARNINGS

Salaries vary greatly within the career and vocational counseling field. The U.S. Department of Labor (DOL) places career counselors within the category of educational, vocational, and school counselors. The median yearly earnings for this group were $52,550 in 2009, according to the DOL. The lowest paid 10 percent of these workers earned $31,140 or less per year, and the highest paid 10 percent made $84,080 or more annually. The department further broke down salaries by type of employer: those working for elementary and secondary schools had mean annual incomes of $61,190 in 2009; for junior colleges, $56,130; for colleges, universities, and professional schools, $49,050; for vocational rehabilitation services, $39,170; and for individual and family services, $37,420. Annual earnings of career counselors vary greatly among educational institutions, with larger institutions offering the highest salaries. Counselors in business or industry tend to earn higher salaries.

In private practice, the salary range is even wider. Some practitioners earn as little as $20,000 per year, and others, such as elite "headhunters" who recruit corporate executives and other high-salaried positions, earn in excess of $100,000 per year.

Salaries for career guidance technicians vary according to education and experience and the geographic location of the job. According to the DOL, social and human services assistants, a job category that includes those employed in vocational rehabilitation services, earned salaries from less than $18,300 to $44,760 or more in 2009, with median annual earnings of $27,940. In general, technicians who are graduates of two-year post–high school training programs can expect to receive starting salaries averaging $20,000 to $25,000 a year. Experienced technicians can earn up to $40,000 annually.

Benefits depend on the employer, but they usually include paid holidays and vacation time, retirement plans, and, for those at some educational institutions, reduced tuition.

## WORK ENVIRONMENT

Employment counselors usually work about 40 hours a week, but some agencies are more flexible. Counseling is done in offices designed to be free from noise and distractions, to allow confidential discussions with clients.

College career planning and placement counselors also normally work a 40-hour week, although irregular hours and overtime are frequently required during the peak recruiting period. They generally work on a 12-month basis.

Career guidance technicians work in very pleasant surroundings, usually in the career services office of a college or vocational school. They will interact with a great number of students, some of whom are eagerly looking for work, and others who are more tense and anxious. The technician must remain unruffled in order to ease any tension and provide a quiet atmosphere.

## OUTLOOK

Employment in the field of employment counseling is expected to grow faster than the average for all occupations through 2018, according to the U.S. Department of Labor. One reason for this steady growth is increased school enrollments, even at the college level, which means more students needing the services of career counselors. Opportunities should also be available in government agencies as many states institute welfare-to-work programs or simply cut welfare benefits. And finally, in this age of outsourcing and lack of employment security, "downsized" workers, those reentering the workforce, and those looking for second careers all create a need for the skills of career and employment counselors.

# FOR MORE INFORMATION

*For a variety of career resources for career seekers and career counseling professionals, contact the following organizations:*
American Counseling Association
5999 Stevenson Avenue
Alexandria, VA 22304-3304
Tel: 800-347-6647
http://www.counseling.org

Career Planning & Adult Development Network
543 Vista Mar Avenue
Pacifica, CA 94044-1951
Tel: 650-359-6911
E-mail: admin@careernetwork.org
http://www.careernetwork.org

*For resume and interview tips, general career information, and advice from experts, contact or visit the following Web site:*
National Association of Colleges and Employers
62 Highland Avenue
Bethlehem, PA 18017-9481
Tel: 800-544-5272
http://www.naceweb.org

*For information on certification, contact*
National Board for Certified Counselors
3 Terrace Way
Greensboro, NC 27403-3660
Tel: 336-547-0607
E-mail: nbcc@nbcc.org
http://www.nbcc.org

*For more information on career counselors, contact*
National Career Development Association
305 North Beech Circle
Broken Arrow, OK 74012-2293
Tel: 918-663-7060
http://ncda.org

# Child Life Specialists

## QUICK FACTS

**School Subjects**
Health
Psychology

**Personal Skills**
Communication/ideas
Helping/teaching

**Work Environment**
Primarily indoors
Primarily one location

**Minimum Education Level**
Bachelor's degree

**Salary Range**
$31,810 to $44,212 to
$56,972+

**Certification or Licensing**
Recommended

**Outlook**
About as fast as the average

**DOT**
195

**GOE**
12.02.02

**NOC**
N/A

**O*NET-SOC**
21-1021.00

## OVERVIEW

*Child life specialists* work in health care settings to help infants, children, adolescents, and their families through illness or injury. One of the primary roles of the child life specialist is to ease the anxiety and stress that often accompany hospitalization, injury, or routine medical care. Child life specialists help children, adolescents, and their families maintain living patterns that are as close to normal as possible, and they try to minimize the potential trauma of hospitalization. Child life specialists do this by providing opportunities for play and relaxation, interaction with other children, and personalized attention. They also encourage family involvement, which can play a major role in helping children and adolescents cope with difficult situations. Child life specialists may help children and their families to develop coping skills and educate them about the experience that they are going through. They may also work with children of adult patients.

Some hospitals refer to their child life specialists as play therapists, patient activity therapists, activity therapists, or therapeutic recreation specialists.

## HISTORY

At one time physicians and nurses were the only adults responsible for the care of children in hospitals. Parents left their children in hospitals, frequently for long periods of time, for treatment of their illnesses. But many parents felt that their children's emotional needs were not being met. Children were often not told about what tests, treatments, or procedures they were to undergo, and as a result their hospital experience was frequently traumatic. In addition, social workers who were part

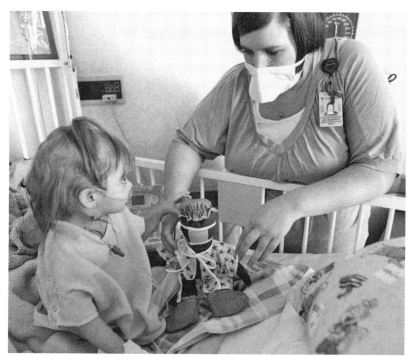

A child life specialist hands a two-year-old girl a "respiratory buddy" as she receives treatment for cystic fibrosis. *(Fernando Salazar, AP Photo/ The Wichita Eagle)*

of the health care team sometimes were not specially trained to work with children and could not provide them with support.

During the early 20th century attempts were made to improve health care workers' understanding of children's needs and to make hospital stays less emotionally difficult for children. C. S. Mott Hospital in Ann Arbor, Michigan, for example, created the nation's first child life department, focusing on child development, in 1922. Gradually, during the 1940s and 1950s, "play programs" were developed at various care facilities across the country. In these settings children were allowed to relax, play, and feel safe. As professional interest in and understanding of child development grew, the play programs began to be seen not only as a play time but also as a therapeutic part of children's care during hospital stays. During the 1960s and 1970s, the field of child life grew dramatically as it gained increasing acceptance.

The profession of child life specialists was formally recognized in 1974, when the Association for the Care of Children's Health formed

## Books to Read

Clark, Cindy Dell. *In Sickness and in Play: Children Coping with Chronic Illness*. Piscataway, N.J.: Rutgers University Press, 2003.

Hubbuck, Catherine. *Play for Sick Children: Play Specialists in Hospitals and Beyond*. London, U.K.: Jessica Kingsley Publishers, 2009.

Oremland, Evelyn K., and Jerome D. Oremland. (eds.) *Protecting the Emotional Development of the Ill Child: The Essence of the Child Life Profession*. Madison, Conn.: Psychosocial Press, 2000.

Thompson, Richard H. *The Handbook of Child Life: A Guide for Pediatric Psychosocial Care*. Springfield, Ill.: Charles C. Thomas Publisher, 2009.

a committee for child life and activity specialists. The committee, which became the independent organization Child Life Council (CLC) in 1982, had as its goals to promote the profession of child life specialist as well as to strengthen these specialists' professional identity. The committee's members recognized that the interruption of a hospitalization or even an ambulatory procedure can have negative consequences for children's growth and development. Today, child life specialists are recognized as an integral part of a child's health care team.

## THE JOB

When children are hospitalized, the experience can be frightening. Child life specialists need to be tuned into the child's or adolescent's concerns. For some children, separation from their families and the familiarity of home can be traumatic. For others, repeated blood tests, needles, or painful procedures can cause fears or nightmares. Emotional damage can be a danger even for adolescents. No matter how short or long the hospital stay and no matter how serious the illness or injury, children can experience anxiety or other emotional effects.

Child life specialists try to ease the possible trauma of being in the hospital. They play an important role in educating and comforting both the patients and their families. They become familiar and trusted adults, and they are usually the only professionals who do not perform tests on the children.

Child life specialists may use dolls and medical instruments to show children what the doctor will be doing. They may help children act out their concerns by having them give a doll a shot if they receive one. The child life specialist may use recreational activities, art projects, cooking, music, and outdoor play in their work. Programs are tailored to meet the needs of individual patients. Some children are unable to express their fears and concerns and may need the child life specialist to draw them out. Some children rely on the child life specialist to help them understand what is happening to them. Still others need the child life specialist to explain children's emotional outbursts or withdrawal to their families.

When children are hospitalized for a long period of time, child life specialists may accompany them to procedures, celebrate successful treatment, or plan a holiday celebration. Child life specialists may also take children on preadmission orientation and hospital tours. They serve as advocates for children's issues by promoting rooming-in or unrestricted parental or sibling visits. Many child life specialists work in conjunction with local school districts to help children keep up with school while they are in the hospital.

*Child life administrators* supervise child life personnel. In larger facilities, the administrators work with other hospital administrators to run the child life programs smoothly within the hospital setting.

Child life specialists can turn their patients' hospital stays into a time of growth. Children are very resilient, and with proper care by their entire health team, they can emerge from hospital stays with a sense of accomplishment and heightened self-esteem.

# REQUIREMENTS
## High School
If you are interested in becoming a child life specialist, you will need to plan on going to college after high school. Therefore, you should take a college preparatory curriculum. As a child life specialist you will need to understand family dynamics, child development, educational play, and basic medical terminology. To help you prepare for this specialty, take psychology and sociology courses and, if available, child development classes. In addition, be sure that your class schedule includes science courses, including health and biology. Because communication is such an important aspect of this work, take English, communication, and speech classes. You may also want to take art, physical education, and drama classes to develop skills that you can use in a variety of therapies, such as play, art, and recreation therapy.

## Postsecondary Training

Some colleges or universities offer specific programs in child life, and quite a number of schools offer course work in areas related to child life. Those who attend colleges or universities that do not have specific child life programs should major in another appropriate field, such as child development, psychology, or social work. Do some research before you select a school to attend. The CLC advises those considering this career to look for a school program that has sufficient faculty, a variety of field opportunities, and positive student evaluations. The CLC offers a list of undergraduate and graduate child life programs at its Web site, http://www.childlife.org. Typical classes to take include child psychology, child growth and development, family dynamics, and theories of play. Select a program that offers internships. An internship will give you supervised experience in the field as well as prepare you for future employment.

According to a member survey by the Child Life Council, 65 percent of child life specialists reported having a bachelor's degree as their highest educational level.

A child life administrator is usually required to have a master's degree in child development, behavioral psychology, education, or a related field. Graduate-level course work typically includes the areas of administration, research, and advanced clinical issues. Those who wish to be considered for positions as child life administrators must also have work experience supervising staff members, managing budgets, and preparing educational materials.

## Certification or Licensing

Certification as a certified child life specialist is available through the Child Life Council. Certification criteria include having a bachelor's degree, having completed 10 college-level courses in child life or a related department/subject, passing an examination, and completing 480 hours of child life clinical work. Although certification is voluntary, it is highly recommended. Some health care centers will not hire a child life specialist who is not certified.

## Other Requirements

To be a successful child life specialist you should enjoy working with people, especially children. You will be part of a health care team, so you must be able to communicate effectively with medical professionals as well as able to communicate with children and their families. You must be creative in order to come up with different ways to explain complicated events, such as surgery, to a child without frightening him or her. You will also need maturity and emotional stability to deal with situations that may otherwise upset you, such as seeing chronically ill or severely injured children. Those who enjoy this work are able to focus on its positive aspects—helping children and their families through difficult times.

## EXPLORING

An excellent way to explore your interest in and aptitude for this work is to volunteer. For volunteer opportunities in medical settings, find out what local hospitals, outpatient clinics, or nursing homes have to offer. Opportunities to work with children are also available through organizations such as Easter Seals, Boy Scouts and Girl Scouts, and Big Brothers Big Sisters of America. In addition, volunteer or paid positions are available at many summer camps. Babysitting, of course, is another way to work with children as well as earn extra money. And a good babysitter is always in demand, no matter where you live.

Once you are in college you can join the CLC as a student member. Membership includes a subscription to the council's newsletter, which can give you a better understanding of the work of a child life specialist.

## EMPLOYERS

Child life specialists work as members of the health care team typically in hospitals. Increasingly, though, specialists are finding employment outside of hospitals at such places as outpatient health care facilities, offices of physicians, rehabilitation centers, hospices, and ambulatory care facilities. Other employers include specialized camps, funeral homes, and court systems. Most child life programs in hospitals are autonomous and report to hospital administrations as other departments and programs do.

Child life programs often work with school programs within hospitals. Specialists may work with teachers to coordinate the curriculum with recreational activities. They also may encourage hospital administrations to provide adequate classroom facilities and highly qualified teachers.

## STARTING OUT

Your internship may provide you with valuable contacts that can give you information on job leads. In addition, the career services office of your college or university should be able to help you locate your first job. The Child Life Council offers its members use of a job bank that lists openings at hospitals and clinics. You may also contact the human resources departments of hospitals directly for information on available positions.

## ADVANCEMENT

Becoming certified and keeping up with new developments through continuing education workshops and seminars are the first two steps anyone must take in order to advance in this field. The next step is to get a graduate degree. Advancement possibilities include the positions of child life administrator, assistant director, or director of a child life program. Advanced positions involve management responsibilities, including the overseeing of a staff and coordinating a program's activities. Those in advanced positions must also keep their knowledge up to date through continuing education, attending professional conferences, and reading professional journals.

## EARNINGS

Salaries for child life specialists vary greatly depending on such factors as the region of the country a specialist works in, education level, certification, and the size of the employer. For example, salaries tend to be higher in large metropolitan teaching hospitals than in small community hospitals. According to a member survey by the Child Life Council, child life specialists earned median annual salaries of $39,000 in January 2008. Salaries ranged from less than $35,000 to $43,134 or more. In 2010, a Payscale.com salary survey reported that child life specialists earned from less than $31,810 to more than $56,972 annually, with median salaries of $44,212. Those with the highest earnings are usually child life administrators or directors. In addition, child life specialists with certification tend to earn more than their noncertified counterparts.

Benefits vary by employer, but they usually include such items as paid vacation and sick days, medical insurance, and retirement plans.

## WORK ENVIRONMENT

Child life specialists are members of the health care team in a variety of settings, including hospitals, clinics, and hospice facilities. In most hospitals, the child life specialist works in a special playroom. Sometimes the specialist may go to the child's hospital room. In outpatient facilities, the specialist may work in a waiting room or a designated playroom. According to the American Academy of Pediatrics, the ratio of child life specialists to children that works well is about one to 15. Child life specialists must be comfortable in hospital settings. They need to adjust easily to being around children who are sick. Since the children and their families need so much support, child life specialists need to be emotionally stable. Their own support network of family and friends should be strong, so that the specialist can get through difficult times at work. Child life specialists may have patients who die, and this can be difficult.

Most child life personnel work during regular business hours, although specialists are occasionally needed on evenings, holidays, or weekends to work with children. It is important for child life personnel to have hobbies or outside interests to avoid becoming too emotionally drained from the work. The rewards of a child life specialist career are great. Many child life specialists see the direct effects of their work on their patients and on their patients' families. They see anxiety and fear being eased, and they see their patients come through treatments and hospitalizations with a renewed pride.

## OUTLOOK

The employment outlook for child life specialists is good. The American Academy of Pediatrics reports that most hospitals specializing in pediatric care have child life programs. And although managed-care providers encourage short hospital stays that may result in a reduced need for staffing in hospitals, opportunities for child life specialists are increasing outside of the hospital setting. The possible employers of today and tomorrow include outpatient clinics, rehabilitation centers, hospice programs, and other facilities that may treat children, such as sexual assault treatment centers and centers for abused women and children.

## FOR MORE INFORMATION

*For current news on issues affecting children's health, visit the academy's Web site.*
American Academy of Pediatrics
141 Northwest Point Boulevard
Elk Grove Village, IL 60007-1098
Tel: 847-434-4000
http://www.aap.org

*For education, career, and certification information as well as professional publications, contact*

**Child Life Council**
11821 Parklawn Drive, Suite 310
Rockville, MD 20852-2539
Tel: 301-881-7090
http://www.childlife.org

*For information on children's health issues and pediatric care, contact*

**National Association of Children's Hospitals and**
　**Related Institutions**
401 Wythe Street
Alexandria, VA 22314-1915
Tel: 703-684-1355
http://www.childrenshospitals.net

# Creative Arts Therapists

## OVERVIEW

*Creative arts therapists* treat and rehabilitate people with mental, physical, and emotional disabilities. They use the creative processes of music, art, dance/movement, drama, psychodrama, and poetry in their therapy sessions to determine the underlying causes of problems and to help patients achieve therapeutic goals. Creative arts therapists usually specialize in one particular type of therapeutic activity. The specific objectives of the therapeutic activities vary according to the needs of the patient and the setting of the therapy program.

## HISTORY

Creative arts therapy programs are fairly recent additions to the health care field. Although many theories of mental and physical therapy have existed for centuries, it has been only in the last 75 years or so that health care professionals have truly realized the healing powers of music, art, dance, and other forms of artistic self-expression.

Art therapy is based on the idea that people who cannot discuss their problems with words must have another outlet for self-expression. In the early 1900s, psychiatrists began to look more closely at their patients' artwork, realizing that there could be links between the emotional or psychological illness and the art. Sigmund Freud even did some preliminary research into the artistic expression of his patients.

**QUICK FACTS**

**School Subjects**
Art
Music
Theater/dance

**Personal Skills**
Artistic
Helping/teaching

**Work Environment**
Primarily indoors
Primarily one location

**Minimum Education Level**
Master's degree

**Salary Range**
$18,000 to $50,000 to $77,000

**Certification or Licensing**
Recommended (certification)
Required by certain states (licensing)

**Outlook**
Faster than the average

**DOT**
076

**GOE**
14.06.01

**NOC**
3144

**O*NET-SOC**
29–1125.00

In the 1930s, art educators discovered that children often expressed their thoughts better with pictures and role-playing than they did through verbalization. Children often do not know the words they need to explain how they feel or how to make their needs known to adults. Researchers began to look into art as a way to treat children who were traumatized by abuse, neglect, illness, or other physical or emotional disabilities.

During and after World War II, the Department of Veterans Affairs (VA) developed and organized various art, music, and dance activities for patients in VA hospitals. These activities had a dramatic effect on the physical and mental well-being of World War II veterans, and creative arts therapists began to help treat and rehabilitate patients in other health care settings.

Because of early breakthroughs with children and veterans, the number of arts therapists has increased greatly over the past few decades, and the field has expanded to include drama, psychodrama, and poetry, in addition to the original areas of music, art, and dance. Today, creative arts therapists work with diverse populations of patients in a wide range of facilities (from small children to senior citizens), and they focus on the specific needs of a vast spectrum of disorders and disabilities. Colleges and universities offer degree programs in many types of therapies, and national associations for registering and certifying creative arts therapists work to monitor training programs and to ensure the professional integrity of the therapists working in the various fields.

# THE JOB

Tapping a power related to dreaming, creative arts therapy taps into the subconscious and gives people a mode of expression in an uncensored environment. This is important because before patients can begin to heal, they must first identify their feelings. Once they recognize their feelings, they can begin to develop an understanding of the relationship between their feelings and their behavior.

The main goal of a creative arts therapist is to improve the client's physical, mental, and emotional health. Before therapists begin any treatment, they meet with a team of other health care professionals, such as nurses, physicians, physical therapists, and social workers. After determining the strength, limitations, and interests of their client, they create a program to promote positive change and growth. The creative arts therapist continues to confer with the other health care workers as the program progresses, and alters the program according to the client's progress. How these goals are reached depends on the unique specialty of the therapist in question.

Creative arts therapists work with all age groups: young children, adolescents, adults, and senior citizens. They can work in individual, group, or family sessions. The approach of the therapist, however, depends on the specific needs of the client or group. For example, if an individual is feeling overwhelmed by too many options or stimuli, the therapist may give him or her only a plain piece of paper and a pencil to work with that day. A music therapist working with a stroke victim would first assess his or her current level of functioning and physical and mental health before and after the stroke and establish short- and long-term goals to regain and improve functioning. Therapists who work with the elderly must accept the fact that a patient may never completely recover or only show marginal improvement.

To reach their patients, creative arts therapists can use a variety of mediums, including visual art, music, dance, drama, or poetry or other kinds of creative writing. Creative arts therapists use many tools in their sessions, including clay, chalk, paint, musical instruments, or paper. Therapists themselves are perhaps the most important tool. They have to use their eyes and ears to pay constant attention to the behavior of patients before, during, and after the session. That behavior is as important as the art work that they create.

Creative arts therapists usually specialize in a specific practice area, becoming a music therapist, art therapist, dance therapist, drama therapist, or poetry therapist.

*Music therapists* use musical lessons and activities to improve a patient's self-confidence and self-awareness, to relieve states of depression, and to improve physical dexterity or mental acuity. For example, a music therapist treating a patient with Alzheimer's might play songs from the patient's past in order to stimulate long- and short-term memory, soothe feelings of agitation, and increase a sense of reality.

*Art therapists* use art in much the same manner. The art therapist may encourage and teach patients to express their thoughts, feelings, and anxieties via sketching, drawing, painting, or sculpting.

*Dance/movement therapists* develop and conduct dance/movement sessions to help improve the physical, mental, and emotional health of their patients. Dance and movement therapy is also used as a way of assessing a patient's progress toward reaching therapeutic goals.

*Drama therapists* use role-playing, pantomime (the telling of a story by the use of expressive body or facial movements), puppetry,

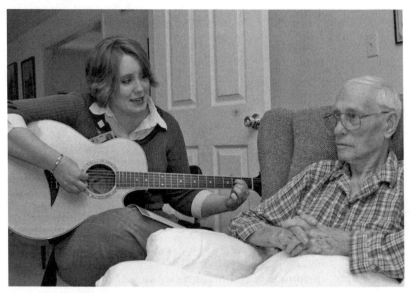

A music therapist performs a song for a hospice patient. (*Cecil Whig, Adelma Gregory-Bunnell, AP Photo*)

improvisation, and original scripted dramatization to evaluate and treat patients.

*Poetry therapists* and *bibliotherapists* use the written and spoken word to treat patients.

## REQUIREMENTS

### High School

To become a creative arts therapist, you will need a bachelor's degree, so take a college preparatory curriculum while in high school. You should become as proficient as possible with the methods and tools related to the type of creative arts therapy you wish to pursue. When therapists work with patients they must be able to concentrate completely on the patient rather than on learning how to use tools or techniques. For example, if you want to become involved in music therapy, you need to be familiar with musical instruments as well as theory. A good starting point for a music therapist is to study piano or guitar.

In addition to courses such as drama, art, music, and English, you should consider taking an introductory class in psychology. Also, a communication class will give you an understanding of the various ways people communicate, both verbally and nonverbally.

## Postsecondary Training

To become a creative arts therapist you must earn at least a bachelor's degree, usually in the area in which you wish to specialize. For example, those studying to be art therapists typically have undergraduate degrees in studio art, art education, or psychology with a strong emphasis on art courses as well.

In most cases, however, you will also need a graduate degree before you can gain certification as a professional or advance in your chosen field. Requirements for admission to graduate schools vary by program, so you would be wise to contact the graduate programs you are interested in to find out about their admissions policies. For some fields you may be required to submit a portfolio of your work along with the written application. Professional organizations can be a good source of information regarding high-quality programs. For example, both the American Art Therapy Association and the American Music Therapy Association provide lists of schools that meet their standards for approval. (Contact information for both associations is listed at the end of this article.)

In graduate school, your study of psychology and the arts field you are interested in will be in-depth. Classes for someone seeking a master's in art therapy, for example, may include group psychotherapy, foundation of creativity theory, assessment and treatment planning, and art therapy presentation. In addition to classroom study you will also complete an internship or supervised practicum (that is, work with clients). Depending on your program, you may also need to write a thesis or present a final artistic project before receiving your degree.

## Certification or Licensing

Typically, the nationally recognized association or certification board specific to your field of choice offers registration and certification. For example, the Art Therapy Credentials Board (ATCB) offers registration and certification to art therapists, and the American Dance Therapy Association offers certification to dance therapists. In general, requirements for registration include completing an approved therapy program and having a certain amount of experience working with clients. Requirements for higher levels of registration or certification generally involve having additional work experience and passing a written exam.

For a specific example, consider the certification process for an art therapist: An art therapist may receive the designation of art therapist registered from the ATCB after completing a graduate program and having some experience working with clients. The next level, then, is to become a board-certified art therapist by passing a written exam. To retain certification status, therapists must complete a certain amount of continuing education.

Many registered creative arts therapists also hold additional licenses in other fields, such as social work, education, mental health, or marriage and family therapy. In some states, creative arts therapists need licensing depending on their place of work. For specific information on licensing in your field, you will need to check with your state's licensing board. Creative arts therapists are also often members of other professional associations, including the American Psychological Association, the American Association for Marriage and Family Therapy, and the American Counseling Association.

## Other Requirements

To succeed in this line of work, you should have a strong desire to help others seek positive change in their lives. All types of creative arts therapists must be able to work well with other people—both patients and other health professionals—in the development and implementation of therapy programs. You must have the patience and the stamina to teach and practice therapy with patients for whom progress is often very slow because of their various physical and emotional disorders. A therapist must always keep in mind that even a tiny amount of progress might be extremely significant for some patients and their families. A good sense of humor is also a valuable trait.

## EXPLORING

There are many ways to explore the possibility of a career as a creative arts therapist. Contact professional associations for information on therapy careers. Talk with people working in the creative arts therapy field and perhaps arrange to observe a creative arts therapy session. Look for part-time or summer jobs or volunteer at a hospital, clinic, nursing home, or any of a number of health care facilities. These opportunities may help provide insight into the nature of creative arts therapy, including both its rewards and demands. Such experience can be very valuable in deciding if you are suited to the inherent frustrations of a therapy career.

## EMPLOYERS

Creative arts therapists usually work as members of an interdisciplinary health care team that may include physicians, nurses, social workers, psychiatrists, and psychologists. Although often employed in hospitals, therapists also work in rehabilitation centers, nursing homes, day treatment facilities, shelters for battered women, pain and stress management clinics, substance abuse programs, hospices, and correctional facilities. Others maintain their own private practices. Many creative arts therapists work with children in grammar and high schools, either as therapists or art teachers. Some arts therapists teach or conduct research in the creative arts at colleges and universities.

## STARTING OUT

After earning a bachelor's degree in a particular field, you should complete your certification, which may include an internship or assistantship. Unpaid training internships often can lead to a first job in the field. Graduates can use the career services office at their college or university to help them find positions in the creative arts therapy field. Many professional associations also compile lists of job openings to assist their members.

Creative arts therapists who are new to the field might consider doing volunteer work at a nonprofit community organization, correctional facility, or neighborhood association to gain some practical experience. Therapists who want to start their own practice can host group therapy sessions in their homes. Creative arts therapists may also wish to associate with other members of the complementary/alternative health care field in order to gain experience and build a client base.

## ADVANCEMENT

With more experience, therapists can move into supervisory, administrative, and teaching positions. Often, the supervision of interns can resemble a therapy session. The interns will discuss their feelings and ask questions they may have regarding their work with clients. How did they handle their clients? What were the reactions to what their clients said or did? What could they be doing to help more? The supervising therapist helps the interns become competent creative arts therapists.

Many therapists have represented the profession internationally at association or educational conferences. Others write articles and books about creative arts therapy or appear as experts on television and radio. Raising the public and professional awareness of creative arts therapy is an important concern for many therapists.

# EARNINGS

A therapist's annual salary depends on experience, level of training, education, and specialty. Working on a hospital staff or being self-employed also affects annual income. According to the American Art Therapy Association (AATA), entry-level art therapists earn annual salaries of approximately $32,000. Median annual salaries are about $38,000 to $45,000, and AATA reports that top earnings for salaried administrators ranged from $50,000 and $100,000 annually. Those who have Ph.D.'s and are licensed for private practice can earn between $85 and $120 per hour, according to AATA. However, those in private practice must pay professional expenses such as insurance and office rental.

Salaries for music therapists vary based on experience, level of training, and education. Music therapists earned average annual salaries of $46,417 in 2008 according to the AMTA. The average annual salary for music therapists was $46,971 in geriatric facilities and $48,387 in physical rehabilitation facilities. According to MENC: The National Association for Music Education, music therapists earn the following annual salaries based on employment setting: hospital-psychiatric facility, $20,000 to $62,000; mental health center, $21,000 to $65,000; nursing home, $17,000 to $65,000; and private practice, $18,000 to $77,000.

Benefits depend on the employer but generally include paid vacation time, health insurance, and paid sick days. Those who are in private practice must provide their own benefits.

# WORK ENVIRONMENT

Most creative arts therapists work a typical 40-hour, five-day workweek; at times, however, they may have to work extra hours. The number of patients under a therapist's care depends on the specific employment setting. Although many therapists work in hospitals, they may also be employed in such facilities as clinics, rehabilitation centers, children's homes, schools, and nursing homes. Some therapists maintain service contracts with several facilities. For instance, a therapist might work two days a week at a hospital, one day at a nursing home, and the rest of the week at a rehabilitation center.

Most buildings are pleasant, comfortable, and clean places in which to work. Experienced creative arts therapists might choose to be self-employed, working with patients in their own studios. In such a case, the therapist might work more irregular hours to accommodate patient schedules. Other therapists might maintain a combination of service contract work with one or more facilities in addition to a private caseload of clients referred to them by other health care professionals. Whether therapists work on service contracts with various facilities or maintain private practices, they must deal with all of the business and administrative details and worries that go along with being self-employed.

## OUTLOOK

The American Art Therapy Association notes that art therapy is a growing field. Demand for new therapists is created as medical professionals and the general public become aware of the benefits gained through art therapies. Although enrollment in college therapy programs is increasing, new graduates are usually able to find jobs. In cases where an individual is unable to find a full-time position, a therapist might obtain service contracts for part-time work at several facilities.

The American Music Therapy Association predicts a promising future for the field of music therapy. Demand for music therapists will grow as medical professionals and the general public become aware of the benefits gained through music therapy.

Job openings in facilities such as nursing homes should continue to increase as the elderly population grows over the next few decades. Advances in medical technology and the recent practice of early discharge from hospitals should also create new opportunities in managed care facilities, chronic pain clinics, and cancer care facilities. The demand for therapists of all types should continue to increase as more people become aware of the need to help disabled patients in creative ways. Some drama therapists and psychodramatists are also finding employment opportunities outside of the usual health care field. Such therapists might conduct therapy sessions at corporate sites to enhance the personal effectiveness and growth of employees.

## FOR MORE INFORMATION

*For more detailed information about your field of interest, contact the following organizations:*
American Art Therapy Association
225 North Fairfax Street
Alexandria, VA 22314-2646
Tel: 888-290-0878
E-mail: info@arttherapy.org
http://www.arttherapy.org

**American Dance Therapy Association**
10632 Little Patuxent Parkway, Suite 108
Columbia, MD 21044-3263
Tel: 410-997-4040
E-mail: info@adta.org
http://www.adta.org

**American Music Therapy Association**
8455 Colesville Road, Suite 1000
Silver Spring, MD 20910-3392
Tel: 301-589-3300
E-mail: info@musictherapy.org
http://www.musictherapy.org

**American Society of Group Psychotherapy and Psychodrama**
301 North Harrison Street, Suite 508
Princeton, NJ 08540-3512
Tel: 609-737-8500
E-mail: asgpp@asgpp.org
http://www.asgpp.org

**National Association for Drama Therapy**
44365 Premier Plaza, Suite 220
Ashburn, VA 20147-5058
Tel: 571-333-2991
E-mail: answers@nadt.org
http://www.nadt.org

**National Association for Poetry Therapy**
Center for Education, Training & Holistic Approaches
777 East Atlantic Avenue, #243
Delray Beach, FL 33483-5360
Tel: 866-844-6278
http://www.poetrytherapy.org

*For an overview of the various types of art therapy, visit the coalition's Web site.*
**National Coalition of Creative Arts Therapies Associations**
c/o American Music Therapy Association
8455 Colesville Road, Suite 1000
Silver Spring, MD 20910-3392
Tel: 201-224-9146
http://www.nccata.org

# Geriatric Social Workers

## OVERVIEW

Geriatric social workers, also known as gerontology social workers, help elderly people adjust to the challenges of growing older. They develop programs and direct agencies that offer counseling, advocacy, and special services. They evaluate the needs of clients and help them arrange for such things as meal service, housing, transportation, and legal and medical assistance. Geriatric social workers also develop recreation and educational programs for the elderly.

Approximately one-third of all social workers work with older people. They work in hospitals, nursing homes, and retirement communities; they have offices in human service agencies and senior centers. Geriatric social workers must have a genuine interest in the well-being of older people and must be sensitive to their concerns and problems.

## HISTORY

Social workers were often the villains of old movies. They were often portrayed as either stiff, unemotional women carrying briefcases and wearing long dark skirts, or as thin, bald men with beady eyes behind thick glasses. With little emotion, they dragged children off to orphanages, committed sane people to insane asylums, and threatened the poor and elderly. The goal of the social worker seemed to be to uphold social norms by breaking up unconventional families. This may reflect a moral superiority that tainted social work up until the early 20th

## QUICK FACTS

**School Subjects**
Psychology
Sociology

**Personal Skills**
Helping/teaching
Leadership/management

**Work Environment**
Primarily indoors
Primarily multiple locations

**Minimum Education Level**
Bachelor's degree

**Salary Range**
$24,940 to $46,300 to $71,190+

**Certification or Licensing**
Recommended (certification)
Required by all states (licensing)

**Outlook**
Much faster than the average

**DOT**
195

**GOE**
12.02.02

**NOC**
4152

**O*NET-SOC**
21-1021.00, 21-1022.00, 21-1023.00, 21-1029.00

century. Today, the social services industry is responsible for empowering individuals (such as the poor, elderly, and ill) and helping them to face personal problems and address large social issues.

Theories and methodologies of social work have changed over the years, but the basis of the profession has remained the same: helping people address hardships such as poverty, illness, drug addictions, and aging. As society changes, so do its problems, calling for redefinition of the social work profession. The U.S. population is getting older. Changing demographics have created a need for experienced professionals in geriatrics. Geriatric social workers help older individuals and their families to cope with the difficulties encountered in aging, such as maintaining mental and physical health and overcoming feelings of depression or fears of dying.

## THE JOB

A woman in her late 70s has just lost her husband and now must live alone for the first time in many years. She has decided to move to another town to live closer to her children and will need help making the transition. She needs a smaller, more manageable home; she needs help with meals and shopping; she would like to make friends in the community. A number of services are available to her, but she may not find out about them without the aid of a geriatric social worker.

As with any social worker, the geriatric social worker is devoted to helping people and communities solve problems. Social workers are dedicated to empowering people and helping people to preserve their dignity and feeling of worth. This kind of assistance and advocacy is especially important among older people. Because old age can sometimes put a person in poor physical and mental health as well as cause financial difficulties, older people often need help and protection. They may need help with preparing meals, finding transportation, and doing housework, or they may need assistance moving into a retirement community or nursing home. But the elderly population of any community is diverse; some older people stay in perfectly good health, and they rely on social services for recreation, meeting people, educational programs, and grief and loss counseling.

People are living longer these days, and the elderly population is growing. At the beginning of the 20th century, only one-half of newborns would live past the age of 50; people born at the beginning of the 21st century can, on average, expect to live well past the age of 75. This is why geriatric social work will continue to offer many job opportunities.

The social work profession is divided into two areas: direct practice and indirect practice. Direct practice is also known as clinical practice. As the name suggests, direct practice involves working directly with the client by offering counseling, advocacy, information and referral, and education. Indirect practice (a practice consisting mostly of social workers who hold Ph.D.'s) concerns the structures through which the direct practice is offered. Indirect practice involves program development and evaluation, administration, and policy analysis. Geriatric social workers may work directly with the elderly population through counseling, advising, and conducting group sessions. They also help clients find services for health, housing, finances, and transportation. Those geriatric social workers involved in indirect practice develop and oversee the agencies and departments that provide these social services.

Geriatric social workers work for service agencies, hospitals, nursing homes, senior centers, and other community organizations. Some also work independently. Their help is needed in every town and city across the country; some social workers in areas with smaller populations may serve a number of small towns within a region. No matter where a geriatric social worker serves, the nature of the work is usually the same. Geriatric social workers meet with older people individually to determine their needs. Home meal delivery programs, transportation services, and recreational programs are some of the basic services offered by community organizations. Some organizations also offer home health care. With nurses and aides assigned to visit the elderly in their homes and to help them with their housework and medical needs, elderly clients can continue to live on their own.

Geriatric social workers evaluate clients by interviewing them and determining their needs; social workers then enroll clients for these services. They make phone calls and provide the service agencies with client information.

The client may need even more assistance. Adult day care services are available in some cities, as are adult foster care services that match older people with families. A social worker may also need to help a client arrange to move into a nursing home and counsel the client about the transition. These counseling services are also extended to members of the client's family, advising them in how to deal with a parent's or grandparent's aging or illness.

In some cases, an elderly person is neglected or taken advantage of. A geriatric social worker can look into these cases and serve as an advocate, stepping in to advise the client of his or her legal rights. In addition to legal services, a geriatric social worker will help a client locate any needed financial services. Social workers help clients make arrangements for the payment of services through Medicare and other financial aid.

Because of efforts by the government to improve the quality of nursing home care, social workers are becoming more active within these facilities. These geriatric social workers work closely with the elderly and their families in arranging the move into the nursing home. They also counsel families upon the death of an elderly relative and help with funeral arrangements. Geriatric social workers also protect and promote the rights of the residents, and they may train nursing care staff members on patient rights.

The geriatric social worker is part of the larger field of aging. This field, which works to provide help for older people while researching the process of aging, is composed of hospitals, health care corporations, government agencies, churches, colleges, and other organizations and institutions. Various professions, such as law, psychology, health care, education, and marketing, include specialties in aging, or gerontology.

## REQUIREMENTS

### High School

Since you will need at least a bachelor's degree to advance in this field, prepare by taking a college prep curriculum in high school. This should include math, science, and computer science classes. Other courses that will help you in this field include civics or government courses, in which you can learn about the enactment of laws, such as the Older Americans Act. Psychology and sociology courses will help you gain an understanding of human behavior and the process of aging as well as teach you methods for studying groups of people, such as the elderly. Take English classes to develop your writing, speaking, and researching skills—skills that you will need throughout your career.

### Postsecondary Training

A minimum of a bachelor's degree in social work, psychology, sociology, or a related field is required for employment as a geriatric social worker, although many employers now require applicants to have a master's degree. The Council on Social Work Education, which accredits bachelor's and master's programs in social work, has approved 468 programs granting the bachelor's degree in social work (B.S.W.) and 196 programs granting the master's degree (M.S.W.). The council offers a listing of member programs at its Web site, http://www.cswe.org. The Group for the Advancement of Doctoral Education in Social Work (http://www.gadephd.org) provides contact information for more than 70 programs that offer the doctor of social work (D.S.W.) degree or the Ph.D. in social work. Accredited B.S.W. programs include courses in human behavior and the social environment, social welfare policy and services, social work practice, research, and field practicum. Most programs require two years of liberal arts study, followed by two years of study in the social work major. Students must also complete a field practicum of at least 400 hours.

Although no clear lines of classification are drawn in the social work profession, most supervisory and administrative positions require at least a master's degree in social work. Master's programs are organized according to fields of practice (such as mental health care), problem areas (substance abuse), population groups (the elderly), and practice roles (practice with individuals, families, or communities). They are usually two-year programs, requiring at least 900 hours of field practice.

Doctoral degrees are usually necessary for research and teaching. Many social workers with doctorates work in community organizations.

## Certification or Licensing
The National Association of Social Workers (NASW) offers certification in several areas. All social workers who meet requirements, which include education, experience, and passing an exam, may receive the designation academy of certified social workers. In addition, the NASW offers specialty certifications, and certification as a qualified clinical social worker and as a diplomate in clinical social work to those who meet specific education, practice, and other requirements. Although certification is voluntary, it is highly recommended for anyone wanting to advance in the field. Certification demonstrates that you have gained the knowledge and experience necessary to meet national standards.

The practice of social work is regulated in all states and the District of Columbia. To receive the necessary licensing, a social worker typically has to gain a certain amount of experience and pass an exam. Because requirements vary by state, you will need to check with the regulatory board in your state for specific information. Licensing information is also available from the Association of Social Work Boards.

## Other Requirements
To be a successful geriatric social worker, you must care about the needs and problems of older people. Many of these people will be relying on you to help them through crucial and difficult times; you

must be completely dedicated to your clients and devoted to helping them maintain their dignity and sense of self-worth.

Most geriatric social workers are involved directly with the people they serve, and they are expected to carefully examine a client's living habits and family relations. A geriatric social worker has to be prepared to confront depressing situations occasionally. In most cases, though, a good geriatric social worker will take pleasure from helping a client through a rough time and will take pride in seeing the client improve his or her life. It is also important for a geriatric social worker to be good-natured and friendly; clients resistant to change may refuse to cooperate with someone they find unpleasant. A geriatric social worker must be very sensitive to the problems of the elderly but must also remain supportive and encouraging.

## EXPLORING

Ask a counselor or teacher to arrange an information interview with a geriatric social worker. Read books and magazines about geriatric care. Volunteering is one of the best ways to explore your interest in geriatric social work. Check with nursing homes, senior care centers, or organizations such as Meals on Wheels in your area for volunteer opportunities. Another way to gain experience is to get summer or part-time work at a local hospital, nursing home, or home health care agency. Home health care aides have the opportunity to work closely with the elderly and to get to know their needs and concerns. Also, as a college student enrolled in a social work program, you may have the opportunity to help a faculty member with a gerontological research project.

## EMPLOYERS

Opportunities for geriatric social workers can be found in both the public and private sectors. Hospitals, nursing homes, retirement communities, human services offices, senior centers, and government agencies all employ geriatric social workers. With so many services available for older people, there are a variety of job opportunities for the geriatric social worker. There are some agencies that deal only with the practical aspects of aiding older people, such as arranging for services and managing financial and legal issues. Working for other agencies may involve the organization of recreational and educational activities, such as senior theater groups and art classes.

## STARTING OUT

After receiving your social work degree and gaining some field experience, you will have made valuable connections among faculty and social service organizations. These connections may be able to help you find a job. Your college's career services office or internship program may also direct you to your first full-time position. You should also become familiar with the local senior centers and agencies for the elderly.

Joining a professional organization can be helpful in entering the field. The American Society on Aging (http://www.asaging.org) sponsors a job bank and publishes newsletters. Job opportunities are listed in the newsletters and at the Web sites of the American Geriatrics Society (http://www.americangeriatrics.org) and other professional organizations. You should also attend annual meetings, which give you the chance to meet other people working in social work, geriatrics, and gerontology.

## ADVANCEMENT

Most geriatric social workers enter the field focusing on the work rather than on the promotions and salary raises. However, there are advancement opportunities for dedicated social workers. Successful social workers may move up the ranks of their organizations to become supervisors or directors, taking on additional responsibilities such as overseeing new hires. A key factor in achieving the most advanced positions is to have advanced education. Those who move into the higher paid positions in administration, program development, or policy analysis must have a Ph.D. or, in some cases, a master's degree with practical experience.

Within smaller agencies and in smaller towns, advancement opportunities may be few, but there may also be less competition for these jobs. A greater number of advancement opportunities may be available in service organizations in urban areas.

## EARNINGS

The U.S. Department of Labor reports that the median annual earnings of medical and public health social workers, a group that includes geriatric social workers, were $46,300 in 2009. The lowest paid 10 percent made less than $28,600, and the highest paid 10 percent made more than $71,190. Social workers working in nursing care facilities earned mean annual salaries of $43,630. Those employed in home health care services earned $49,870.

Median annual earnings for substance abuse and mental health social workers, a category that also includes geriatric social workers, were $38,200 in 2009. Salaries ranged from less than $24,940 to $62,760 or more annually.

Social workers' benefits depend on the employer, but they generally include health insurance and paid vacation time.

## WORK ENVIRONMENT

Although geriatric social workers do spend some time in an office setting, they spend much of their time interviewing clients and the directors of programs; they also visit the homes of their clients to evaluate and take notes. They may also visit the homes of clients' families. Although some geriatric social workers may work in hospital and nursing home environments, others have their offices in human service agencies alongside other service providers. Serving as an advocate for the elderly client requires, in addition to phone calls, e-mails, and faxes, personal meetings with directors of agencies, local legislators, and others. In cases of abuse and neglect, it may require testifying in court.

Because poverty and illness afflict a large number of people over the age of 65, the geriatric social worker is often assigned depressing, seemingly hopeless cases. This may be the situation only temporarily, however, as the social worker introduces the client to the necessary services and assistance.

## OUTLOOK

Employment for social workers is expected to grow faster than the average for all careers through 2018, according to the U.S. Department of Labor (DOL). Job opportunities for medical and public health social workers will be even better, with much faster than average growth predicted. Opportunities are expected to be strongest for social workers employed in assisted-living and senior-living communities. There will also be many jobs in nursing homes, long-term care facilities, and hospices, but the DOL says employment will not be as strong in these settings because other workers are often hired to handle duties typically assigned to social workers. Those specializing in geriatric social work in particular will be in great demand for several reasons. It is estimated that as people live longer more geriatric social workers will be needed to create programs and provide services for the growing number of elderly persons. Rising health care costs are causing many insurance companies to consider alternatives to hospital treatment, so some insurance coverage now includes home stays. In addition, hospitals and nursing homes are trying to balance the demand for their services and their limitations in staff and physical facilities. As home care becomes a viable, affordable option for more older people, more geriatric social workers will be necessary to evaluate the needs of clients and set up services.

The Omnibus Budget Reconciliation Act passed by the U.S. Congress to improve nursing home care requires large nursing care facilities to employ full-time social workers. As the government becomes more involved in providing better care for the elderly, geriatric social workers will see more full-time job opportunities in nursing homes and hospitals.

## FOR MORE INFORMATION

*For more information on careers in geriatric social work, contact*
**American Association of Homes and Services for the Aging**
2519 Connecticut Avenue, NW
Washington, DC 20008-1520
Tel: 202-783-2242
E-mail: info@aahsa.org
http://www.aahsa.org

*For general information on geriatric care, contact*
**American Geriatrics Society**
350 Fifth Avenue, Suite 801
New York, NY 10118-0801
Tel: 212-308-1414
E-mail: info@americangeriatrics.org
http://www.americangeriatrics.org

*For information on continuing education programs, job listings, and student resources, check out the following Web site:*
**American Society on Aging**
71 Stevenson Street, Suite 1450
San Francisco, CA 94105-2938
Tel: 415-974-9600
E-mail: info@asaging.org
http://www.asaging.org

*To read articles about geriatric care–related issues, visit the association's Web site.*
**Association for Gerontology Education in Social Work**
http://www.agesw.org

*To read* Careers in Aging, *visit the association's Web site.*
**Association for Gerontology in Higher Education**
1220 L Street, NW, Suite 901
Washington, DC 20005-4018
Tel: 202-289-9806
http://www.aghe.org

*For information on licensing, contact*
**Association of Social Work Boards**
400 South Ridge Parkway, Suite B
Culpeper, VA 22701-3791
Tel: 800-225-6880
http://www.aswb.org

*For information on education and the field of social work, contact*
**Council on Social Work Education**
1701 Duke Street, Suite 200
Alexandria, VA 22314-3457
Tel: 703-683-8080
E-mail: info@cswe.org
http://www.cswe.org

*For career information and student resources, contact*
**Gerontological Society of America**
1220 L Street NW, Suite 901
Washington, DC 20005-4001
Tel: 202-842-1275
http://www.geron.org

*This organization can provide information on services, including adult day care, available across the country.*
**National Association of Area Agencies on Aging**
1730 Rhode Island Avenue, NW, Suite 1200
Washington, DC 20036-3109
Tel: 202-872-0888
http://www.n4a.org

*For certification information and to read* Choices: Careers in Social Work, *visit the association's Web site.*
**National Association of Social Workers**
750 First Street, NE, Suite 700
Washington, DC 20002-4241
Tel: 202-408-8600
E-mail: membership@naswdc.org
http://www.naswdc.org

# Grief Therapists

## OVERVIEW

A *grief therapist* or *bereavement counselor* offers therapy for those who are mourning the death of a family member or a loved one. Therapists help survivors work through possible feelings of anger or guilt and help them recover from their loss. Counselors may be brought into communities or facilities to help individuals after a national disaster, act of violence, or an accident. Grief therapists may be self-employed as independent counselors or work for hospitals, funeral homes, schools, hospice organizations, nursing homes, or government or private agencies.

## HISTORY

Grief therapy is a relatively new career specialty. According to Dr. Dana Cable, professor of psychology and thanatology at Hood College in Frederick, Maryland, and a certified grief therapist and death educator, "Grief therapy is a growing area because of the nature of many deaths today. There are many more issues to be worked through when we lose young people to violent deaths and diseases such as AIDS. In addition, there is some movement away from organized religion where people used to find comfort when they lost a loved one." Cable also points out that changes in the family unit have affected the way in which family members grieve. Many families are not close, physically or emotionally, resulting in issues of guilt when a family member dies. Other factors that have boosted growth in this field include people's willingness to accept the help of a therapist (something that rarely happened in years past) and the large number

### QUICK FACTS

**School Subjects**
Psychology
Sociology

**Personal Skills**
Communication/ideas
Helping/teaching

**Work Environment**
Primarily indoors
One location with some
travel

**Minimum Education Level**
Master's degree

**Salary Range**
$24,230 to $38,010 to
$64,610+

**Certification or Licensing**
Voluntary (certification)
Required by certain states
(licensing)

**Outlook**
Much faster than the average

**DOT**
195

**GOE**
12.02.02

**NOC**
4153

**O*NET-SOC**
19-3031.03, 21.1014.00

of aging baby boomers who are now beginning to experience the deaths of friends and family members and, thus, have a need for grief therapists' services.

## THE JOB

Grief therapists help individuals accept the death of a spouse, child, partner, parent, sibling, or loved one. Therapists give their clients reassurance and help them examine and resolve feelings, including negative ones, that may be associated with the death. Counseling may be done on a one-to-one basis, with a small group, or as part of a support group.

When disasters such as accidents or violence occur, grief therapists are often brought in to speak to communities, schools, or organizations. They help people deal with the tragedy and may provide individual counseling. In recent times, therapists have been called upon when violence has hit schools, when weather-related tragedies have destroyed communities, and when an airplane has crashed or a terrorist bombing has occurred.

Hospitals, nursing homes, AIDS and cancer care centers, and hospice organizations employ grief therapists to provide emotional support to patients and their families and friends. In addition, some funeral homes refer families and friends to grief therapists as part of an aftercare service following a funeral.

Grief therapists also work as *death educators*. These specialists conduct classes for people who work in professions that deal with the sick and dying, such as medical and nursing students. They may also speak to organizations, clubs, support groups, parents, and others about issues related to death and give them suggestions on how to cope.

## REQUIREMENTS

### High School

College prep classes are essential if you wish to enter the field of grief therapy. In order to learn how to deal with a diverse group of people from all cultural backgrounds, courses in health, sociology, psychology, and religion are helpful. Communication is a key part of the grief therapist's job, so speech, foreign languages, communication, and English courses are also vital. It may be a good idea to check with the colleges you have selected to find out what courses they recommend for a career in psychology and counseling.

## Postsecondary Training
Degrees that feature a strong psychology component or a premed program are usually recommended for counselors. This must be followed with a master's program in counseling, social work, or psychology. Following this with a doctoral degree in psychology is recommended for the best job prospects.

## Certification or Licensing
The Association for Death Education and Counseling offers the certification in thanatology and the fellow in thanatology designations to applicants who meet educational and experiential requirements and pass a multiple-choice examination. Certification must be renewed every three years.

# Where Do Grief Therapists Work?

- Private practice
- Day care centers
- Schools
- Colleges
- Places of worship
- Corporations
- Businesses
- Hospice agencies
- Nursing homes
- Assisted living homes
- Air crash sites
- Hospitals
- Trauma centers
- Cancer care centers
- HIV/AIDS treatment centers
- Industrial accident sites
- Funeral homes
- Natural disaster sites
- Armed forces
- Scenes of violence

Some states require grief therapists to obtain licenses in order to practice. These licensing requirements may vary from state to state, so it is best to check with the state in which you plan to practice. The American Counseling Association also offers detailed information on state licensing requirements for counselors. (See For More Information.) Some states may limit counselors' private practices to areas in which they have developed professional competence. There may also be some continuing education requirements for license renewal.

### Other Requirements

If you are interested in becoming a grief therapist, you should enjoy working with people and feel comfortable dealing with clients who have suffered personal loss. You should show patience and be a compassionate listener, as well as be able to express yourself clearly and tactfully.

Grief therapists must not let their jobs take an emotional toll on their own lives. Though they hear many stories of grief and sadness, therapists can also find their job rewarding and uplifting as they help people overcome feelings of depression and despair and continue with their lives.

## EXPLORING

Your high school counselor may be able to supply information on a career as a therapist. Other sources for information can be found at your local or school library, or through the Internet. Contact the organizations listed at the end of this article for further information.

Doing volunteer work for organizations such as the Red Cross or with your local hospital, nursing home, or hospice care center will give you more experience dealing with the sick, troubled, or grieving. Participating in high school clubs or other groups that organize volunteer projects to benefit homeless people, victims of AIDS, or battered spouses can also give you valuable experience.

## EMPLOYERS

Grief therapists may provide grief therapy as an independent part of their larger counseling practice, or they may work as part of an organization. Many therapists in private practice offer grief therapy. Some therapists are part of a group practice of medical or psychological professionals who offer a variety of counseling and therapy services. Funeral homes, nursing homes, assisted care facilities, AIDS care facilities, hospice organizations, and almost any facility or organization that deals with the sick and dying use grief therapists. Many have a therapist either on call or on staff. The government may also employ counselors and grief therapists in its health care facilities.

Some grief therapists may work under contract with large corporations as part of employee assistance programs. Others may be called upon by airlines, schools, communities, or businesses at times of crisis or when violence has occurred. They may also work on a contract basis to make presentations or seminars to various groups or organizations.

Grief therapists may also work at colleges or universities, conducting research or teaching classes that deal with death and grief.

## STARTING OUT

Some colleges and universities offer job placement for people seeking careers in counseling. While in graduate school, therapy students often work as interns with hospitals, hospices, health care, or crisis care organizations, or with therapists in private practices. These relationships can often offer employment and networking possibilities after graduation.

Most grief therapists practice general counseling before specializing in grief therapy. Building a client base as a counselor can help provide the base for beginning a career in grief therapy. Personal contacts can also provide networking possibilities. Membership in a professional counseling association may offer sources for contacts and help you find job leads. Classified advertisements and trade magazines also list job openings.

## ADVANCEMENT

Counselors specializing in grief therapy can advance to head their own counseling service or group practice, serving clients directly or contracting out services to hospitals, businesses, hospice organizations, and other facilities. Experienced grief therapists who specialize in education can become department heads of universities or colleges. Counselors with a business background and experience can advance to become executive directors of health care facilities, organizations, nursing homes, or head professional organizations that serve the counseling profession.

## EARNINGS

The salary range for grief therapists is generally the same as for other therapists and counselors. According to the U.S. Department of Labor, the median annual salary of mental health counselors was $38,010 in 2009. The lowest paid 10 percent earned less than $24,230, and the highest paid 10 percent earned more than $64,610. Those employed in individual and family services had mean annual earnings of $39,710. Therapists in private practice and those who become directors of facilities may earn considerably more.

Benefits vary depending on the position and the employer but generally vacation, sick leave, insurance, and other work-related benefits are provided. Persons who are self-employed usually have to provide their own insurance and retirement funds.

## WORK ENVIRONMENT

Generally, grief therapists work in office settings that are clean and well lighted. Grief therapists who work in crisis situations will find a wide variety of working environments depending on the situation, but usually small, temporary offices are set up to accommodate counselors.

Counselors in private or group practice may have to set up evening and weekend office hours. Some grief counseling must be done on an emergency basis in times of crisis or violence, so there may be occasions when counselors have to drop everything to work any time of the day or night.

Many counselors stick to a given location to serve the local community. However, depending on the type and range of cases the therapist handles, travel may be necessary, including on nights and weekends.

## OUTLOOK

According to the *Occupational Outlook Handbook,* employment opportunities for mental health counselors (which includes grief therapists) are expected to grow much faster than the average for all occupations through 2018.

A career in grief therapy holds great promise. Our changing and aging society creates a need for grief counseling. As baby boomers age and experience the deaths of their parents, friends, and families, they are seeking the help of bereavement counselors to help them adjust and deal with their feelings. Counseling has become a socially accepted tool to help people deal with difficult or painful situations.

As violent crimes occur and as young people witness acts of violence and experience the untimely death of friends, they seek an understanding that grief counselors can help provide. Car accidents,

AIDS, and drug-related deaths can also create feelings of guilt and depression that counselors can help people work through. Unfortunately, there will continue to be natural disasters such as tornadoes, floods, avalanches, and earthquakes that kill large numbers of people. Grief counselors will continue to be called on to help ease survivors' pain.

Although grief therapists work in every part of the country, demand is highest in retirement areas of the country where there is a large elderly population.

## FOR MORE INFORMATION

*For information on state licensing, certification, accredited graduate programs, and choosing a graduate program, contact*
**American Counseling Association**
5999 Stevenson Avenue
Alexandria, VA 22304-3304
Tel: 800-347-6647
http://www.counseling.org

*For career and certification information, contact*
**Association for Death Education and Counseling**
111 Deer Lake Road, Suite 100
Deerfield, IL 60015-4943
Tel: 847-509-0403
http://www.adec.org

*For information on working with grieving children and their families, contact*
**The Dougy Center for Grieving Children and Families**
PO Box 86852
Portland, OR 97286-0852
Tel: 866-775-5683
E-mail: help@dougy.org
http://www.grievingchild.org

*For information on working with the elderly, contact*
**Gerontological Society of America**
1220 L Street, NW, Suite 901
Washington, DC 20005-4001
Tel: 202-842-1275
http://www.geron.org

*For information on graduate programs in thanatology (the study of grief therapy), contact the following colleges:*

**College of New Rochelle**
Graduate School
29 Castle Place
New Rochelle, NY 10805-2330
Tel: 914-654-5561
E-mail: gs@cnr.edu
http://www.cnr.edu/academics/ProgramsofStudy

**Hood College**
401 Rosemont Avenue
Frederick, MD 21701-8524
Tel: 301-663-3131
http://www.hood.edu/graduate/programs.cfm?pid=programs_
    thanatology_index.html

# HIV/AIDS Counselors and Case Managers

## OVERVIEW

*HIV/AIDS counselors and case managers* work with people who are infected with HIV (human immunodeficiency virus) or have developed AIDS (acquired immunodeficiency syndrome), and with their families and friends, to help them cope with the physical and emotional results of the disease. They answer questions, offer advice and support, and help HIV/AIDS patients get necessary assistance from medical and social agencies.

## HISTORY

No one knows the exact origin of HIV, though there are several different theories. The virus has existed in the United States, Haiti, and Africa since at least 1977 or 1978. In 1979, doctors in Los Angeles and New York began to diagnose and report rare types of pneumonia, cancer, and other illnesses not usually found in persons with healthy immune systems.

The Centers for Disease Control and Prevention (CDC) officially named the condition AIDS (acquired immunodeficiency syndrome) in 1982. In 1984, the virus responsible for weakening the immune system was identified as HIV (human immunodeficiency virus).

Today, the CDC estimates that 1.1 million Americans are living with HIV/AIDS, and more than 56,000 new infections occur each year. The professions of HIV/AIDS counselor and case manager developed in the mid-1980s as a division of social work.

# THE JOB

HIV/AIDS counselors and case managers help HIV and AIDS patients deal with their illness in the best way possible. A person who has tested positive for HIV or who has been diagnosed as having AIDS has to deal with many issues. Some of the issues are similar to those faced by anyone diagnosed with a potentially terminal illness—grief, fear, and concerns over health care, financial planning, and making provisions for children or other family members. Other issues these patients may face are unique to HIV and AIDS sufferers. These may include discrimination, prejudice, and exclusion by family and acquaintances who are afraid of or do not understand the disease. Another special consideration for these patients is how to avoid passing the disease on to others.

Counselors and case managers offer support and assistance in dealing with all the various social, physical, and emotional issues patients face. Together counselors and case managers work with clients in all stages of the disease—from those who have first tested positive for HIV to those who are in the final stages of the illness. They may work at HIV testing centers, public health clinics, mental health clinics, family planning clinics, hospitals, and drug treatment facilities.

Counselors who work at testing facilities, sometimes called *test counselors,* work with individuals who are being tested for HIV. These counselors usually meet with clients before they are tested to find out about the client's level of risk for the disease, to explain the testing procedure, and to talk about what the possible test results mean. They also explain how the HIV infection is spread, discuss ways to prevent it, and answer general questions about the disease and its progress.

Results from the test are typically available a few days to two weeks after the client has had the initial meeting. When the client returns to find out the results, the counselor again meets with him or her. If the results are negative, the counselor may suggest retesting if, during the six months before the test, the client engaged in any behaviors that might have resulted in infection. Since the infection does not show up immediately after it is contracted, it is possible to be infected and still test negative.

If the results are positive, the counselor talks with the client about his or her sexual activity and drug use to determine how they might have gotten the disease. They also help them decide whom to notify of the test results, such as previous sex partners.

At some testing clinics, such as those offering STD (sexually transmitted disease) testing as well as HIV testing, a client initially meets with a nurse who conducts the test. In these circumstances, when the client returns for the test results he or she may then meet with an HIV counselor if necessary.

The counselor is often the first person the HIV-positive client talks to about the illness. A large part of the job, then, is referring the client to appropriate sources of help, including AIDS-related agencies, social services, and health care providers.

Case managers, unlike counselors, follow patients through the various stages of their illness, helping them coordinate and manage the resources necessary to deal with it. In some instances, case managers may not begin working with a client until that client has developed AIDS. Through letters, phone calls, and contacts with a network of available service providers, case managers help their clients get access to the agencies or organizations that offer the assistance they need. Assistance may include medical care, legal help, help with living expenses, or visits by home health care aides.

People with HIV and AIDS are under severe emotional strain. In addition to coping with the physical effects of the disease, they must also cope with the burden of having a disease that much of society does not understand or accept. They may feel anger, depression, guilt, and shame as they learn to live with their disease.

Counselors and case managers help clients deal with these emotional strains. They may conduct AIDS support groups or group counseling sessions in which HIV or AIDS patients discuss their experiences and questions about living with the disease. In these group sessions, the counselor or case manager oversees the conversation and tries to move it in a positive direction.

HIV/AIDS counselors and case managers may also work with the family members, friends, and partners of those with HIV or AIDS, either in individual or group sessions. They may meet with family members or partners to discuss the client's progress or to help them understand their loved one's needs. They may also set up and oversee grief counseling sessions for those who have lost relatives or partners to the disease.

In order to monitor clients' progress, case managers keep written records on each of their sessions. They may be required to participate in staff meetings to discuss a client's progress and treatment plan. They may also meet with members of various social service agencies to discuss their clients' needs.

In addition to the primary duty of counseling clients, these workers may participate in community efforts to increase HIV and AIDS awareness. They may help develop workshops, give speeches to high schools or other groups, or organize and lead public awareness campaigns.

# HIV/AIDS in the United States

- As of the end of 2006, an estimated 1.1 million people were living with diagnosed or undiagnosed HIV/AIDS.
- It is estimated that 56,300 people were diagnosed with HIV/AIDS in 2006.
- Males made up 74 percent of people diagnosed with HIV/AIDS in 2007.
- Twenty-nine percent of those diagnosed with HIV/AIDS in 2007 were between the ages of 13 and 29.
- In 2007, 14,100 people died of AIDS.

Source: Centers for Disease Control and Prevention

## REQUIREMENTS

### High School

If you are considering a career in the field of HIV/AIDS counseling, you should emphasize sociology and psychology classes in your curriculum. Because this area of counseling requires an understanding of how the human body is affected by HIV and AIDS, you should also take classes such as biology, physiology, and health. To develop your communication skills, take English classes. You may also want to take a foreign language, which will give you the ability to communicate with non-English speakers.

### Postsecondary Training

Although specific educational requirements for HIV/AIDS counselors and case managers vary, most employers require a bachelor's degree in mental health, counseling, or social work. Some employers may require their employees to have a master's degree. A college-level curriculum for a degree in mental health or social work is likely to include classes in counseling, sociology, psychology, human development, and mental health. Your college education will also include a minimum of 400 hours of supervised fieldwork, known as a practicum. The Council on Social Work Education (CSWE) is the only accrediting body for bachelor's and master's degree programs in social work in the United States. When selecting a program to attend, make sure it is CSWE approved. To view a listing of such programs, visit http://www.cswe.org/Accreditation/organizations.

aspx. These programs usually last two or two and a half years and require supervised fieldwork of at least 900 hours.

Doctoral degrees are usually necessary for research and teaching. The Group for the Advancement of Doctoral Education in Social Work (http://www.gadephd.org) provides contact information for more than 70 programs that offer the doctor of social work degree or the Ph.D. in social work.

Some employers will hire job candidates with bachelor's degrees in other fields, such as education. To prepare yourself for this work, however, you should include such classes as psychology and health in your course work. Gaining work experience will be essential for you, so look for internships or summer jobs that offer the opportunity to combine your interests, for example in public health education or with an HIV/AIDS service organization. If you cannot find a paid position, you can still strengthen your resume by doing volunteer work at an HIV/AIDS organization; many are involved in such areas as advocacy, education, and home support services.

## Certification or Licensing

Most states require some form of credentialing for HIV/AIDS counselors and case managers. Many choose to be certified by the National Board for Certified Counselors (NBCC). To become certified by the NBCC, candidates must have completed a master's degree in counseling, meet professional experience requirements, and pass a national examination. Upon successful completion of these requirements, the candidate is designated as a national certified counselor. The National Association of Social Workers also offers certification in several areas. Additionally, all states require some form of licensing, registration, or certification for anyone working as a social worker. Requirements vary by state, so you will need to check with your state's licensing board for specific information.

## Other Requirements

Because these diseases receive so much attention from the medical, social, and even government arenas, there are often new developments in HIV- and AIDS-related treatments, policies, and services. In order to keep up to date, counselors and case managers must regularly continue their education by attending seminars or monthly in-service meetings.

For individuals considering a career in HIV/AIDS counseling, certain personal qualifications may be just as important as having the correct educational background. Compassion, sensitivity, and the desire to help others are key qualities for these counselors. They must also be able to communicate effectively and sincerely and to listen with understanding.

HIV/AIDS counselors and case managers must be emotionally stable and resilient in order to keep from becoming depressed and discouraged by the nature of their work. They need to be able to avoid becoming too emotionally involved with their patients by balancing empathy with objectivity.

## EXPLORING

If you are interested in a career in HIV/AIDS counseling, you might contact local hospitals, HIV testing centers, or AIDS service organizations for more information. It may be possible to meet with a counselor to talk about the details of his or her job. Any school or local library should also have a large number of resources both on the AIDS virus and on counseling. You can also use the Internet to get the latest information about HIV and AIDS by visiting such sources as the CDC (http://www.cdc.gov/hiv) and the HIV/AIDS Bureau of the Health Resources and Services Administration (http://www.hab.hrsa.gov).

To further explore the career, you may be able to find a volunteer position in a social service agency, health clinic, or hospital. Even if the position does not deal directly with HIV or AIDS patients, it should provide you with an idea of what it is like to work in such an environment. Once you have graduated from high school, you may be eligible to join the National AIDS Fund AmeriCorps/Caring Counts Program, which trains participants to do HIV/AIDS education and counseling and places them in selected cities. (See the end of this article for the fund's contact information.)

## EMPLOYERS

HIV/AIDS counselors and case managers work for hospitals, hospices, HIV testing centers, public health clinics, mental health clinics, social service agencies, Red Cross offices, Planned Parenthood centers, and various AIDS service organizations. They may also work for regional AIDS consortia organized by health officials, religious leaders, educators, business leaders, and AIDS service representatives.

## STARTING OUT

New graduates may begin their job searches at the career services offices of their colleges. They might also apply directly to any area social service, health, or AIDS service organizations. Some openings for HIV/AIDS counselors or case managers might be advertised in the classified sections of local newspapers. Membership in a professional organization, such as the American Counseling Association, might also provide the job seeker with leads through publications, meetings, or job banks. Additionally, graduates may look for internship opportunities, such as the University of California–San Francisco AIDS Health Project's Post-Baccalaureate Internship Program. This yearlong program offers new college graduates focused education and experience in HIV care. Through such internships, graduates can hone professional skills as well as make professional contacts that may lead to later full-time employment.

## ADVANCEMENT

Counselors and case managers who work for large organizations will have more opportunity for advancement than those who work for smaller ones. In a large organization, for example, the counselor with education and experience might move into an administrative position, such as senior trainer or program director. Because smaller organizations, especially not-for-profit organizations, usually have small staffs, advancement is often slow and limited.

Those who continue their education may have a wider range of possibilities for advancement. Counselors who complete a master's degree in social work or rehabilitative counseling, for example, might be employed by social welfare agencies as medical or psychiatric social workers, child protective workers, rehabilitative counselors, or parole or probation officers. These fields have a broader scope of advancement opportunities.

Finally, some who continue their education elect to go into research or teaching at the college level.

## EARNINGS

Generally, earnings for HIV/AIDS counselors and case managers are similar to those for other counselors and social workers. Salaries can vary, however, depending upon the experience and education of the individual and the location, size, and funding source of the employer. The U.S. Department of Labor reports that medical and public health social workers had median yearly earnings of $46,300 in 2009. The lowest paid 10 percent made less than $28,600 per year, while the highest paid 10 percent earned more than $71,190. Those at the top end of the pay scale typically have extensive experience and advanced degrees and work at well-funded programs.

In addition to salary, most HIV/AIDS counselors and case managers receive a benefits package that includes paid vacations, holidays, and sick time, medical insurance, and sometimes a retirement plan.

## WORK ENVIRONMENT

HIV/AIDS counselors and case managers usually work regular eight-hour days, five days a week. Occasionally, however, they may have appointments with health care providers, social service agencies, or patients outside of regular office hours.

Counselors who work in HIV testing centers and health clinics usually have on-site offices where they can talk privately with clients. Those who work as case managers may visit clients in their homes or in hospitals or other long-range care facilities. They may conduct group sessions in classrooms or conference rooms of hospitals or social service agencies. Regardless of the setting, HIV/AIDS counselors and case managers spend a majority of their day meeting with people—either clients and family members or representatives from social service or health care agencies.

Counseling those with HIV and AIDS is stressful and often depressing work. In many cases, clients are preparing for eventual death, and they turn to the counseling professional for help and support in facing it. Case managers often watch their clients become very sick as the virus progresses; frequently, they must deal with clients' deaths. Dealing with this sickness, death, and the accompanying emotional distress on a daily basis may be difficult.

## OUTLOOK

Employment trends for HIV/AIDS counselors and case managers are likely to depend upon government funding for AIDS-related programs, since private funding for such programs is usually limited. Government funding for health programs, however, fluctuates, and resistance from some special interest groups or policy makers may negatively influence spending on AIDS research and programs. Nevertheless, the U.S. Department of Labor predicts that employment for social workers, who are closely related professionals, will grow faster than the average for all occupations through 2018. Employment of mental health counselors (which often include HIV/AIDS counselors and case managers) is expected to grow much faster than the average during this same time span. Additional factors influencing job opportunities for HIV/AIDS counselors and case managers include the continued spread of HIV, the increased number of people living longer with HIV than in previous years, and the new complications (medical, financial, and even social) that are brought on by new treatments. Given all of these various factors, experts predict that employment for HIV/AIDS counselors will continue to increase.

These professionals can play an especially important role in educating the public at large and those with HIV and AIDS on how to cope with the disease and avoid its spread. Jobs for HIV/AIDS counselors and case managers will probably be most plentiful in urban areas, with their larger populations. Those with the most current knowledge and HIV/AIDS training will find the best opportunities.

## FOR MORE INFORMATION

*For information about counseling and graduate programs in counseling, contact*
American Counseling Association
5999 Stevenson Avenue
Alexandria, VA 22304-3304
Tel: 800-347-6647
http://www.counseling.org

*For information about HIV and AIDS, contact the following organizations:*
Centers for Disease Control and Prevention
1600 Clifton Road
Atlanta, GA 30333
Tel: 800-232-4636 or 800-342-2437 (National AIDS Hotline)
E-mail: cdcinfo@cdc.gov
http://www.cdc.gov/hiv

HIV/AIDS Programs
U.S. Department of Health and Human Services
Health Resources and Services Administration
5600 Fishers Lane
Rockville, MD 20857-0002
Tel: 888-275-4772
E-mail: ask@hrsa.gov
http://www.hab.hrsa.gov

*For information on social work careers, contact*
National Association of Social Workers
750 First Street, NE, Suite 700
Washington, DC 20002-4241
Tel: 202-408-8600

E-mail: membership@naswdc.org
http://www.naswdc.org

*For information about certification, contact*
**National Board for Certified Counselors**
3 Terrace Way
Greensboro, NC 27403-3660
Tel: 336-547-0607
E-mail: nbcc@nbcc.org
http://www.nbcc.org

*For more information on this AmeriCorps program, contact*
**National AIDS Fund AmeriCorps/Caring Counts Program**
729 15th Street, NW, 9th Floor
Washington, DC 20005-1511
Tel: 202-408-4848
http://www.aidsfund.org

# Home Health Care Aides

## OVERVIEW

*Home health care aides,* also known as *homemaker–home health aides* or *home attendants,* serve elderly and infirm persons by visiting them in their homes and caring for them. Working under the supervision of nurses or social workers, they perform various household chores that clients are unable to perform for themselves as well as attend to patients' personal needs. Although they work primarily with the elderly, home health care aides also attend to clients with disabilities or those needing help with small children. There are approximately 921,700 home health aides employed in the United States.

## HISTORY

Family photographs from the last century frequently included a grandparent posed alongside the children or an elderly aunt or uncle arm-in-arm with a niece or nephew. A typical household of the time often counted an elderly parent or ill or injured relative among its members. Without most of the modern conveniences we take for granted today, day-to-day living and regular household chores could be impossible for someone weakened by illness or age. It was often expected for parents to move in with children when they became unable to look after themselves; sometimes a room was prepared and waiting for them long in advance. In rural situations, elderly parents might have been expected to give up the homestead to a child or grandchild once they became incapable of looking after the place themselves.

## QUICK FACTS

**School Subjects**
Family and consumer science
Health

**Personal Skills**
Following instructions
Helping/teaching

**Work Environment**
Primarily indoors
Primarily multiple locations

**Minimum Education Level**
High school diploma

**Salary Range**
$15,950 to $20,480 to $29,390+

**Certification or Licensing**
Required for certain positions

**Outlook**
Much faster than the average

**DOT**
354

**GOE**
14.07.01

**NOC**
3413

**O*NET-SOC**
31-1011.00, 39-9021.00

## Books to Read

Anene, Emmanuel C. *Home Health Aide Training Manual and Handbook*. Bloomington, Ind.: iUniverse, 2009.
Fuzy, Jetta, William Leahy, Susan Alvare, and Thaddeus Castillo. *The Home Health Aide Handbook*. 2d ed. Albuquerque, N.M.: Hartman Publishing Inc., 2005.
Leahy, William, Jetta Fuzy, Julie Grafe, and Susan Alvare. *Providing Home Care: A Textbook for Home Health Aides*. 3d ed. Albuquerque, N.M.: Hartman Publishing Inc., 2008.
Perry, Angela. (ed.) *American Medical Association Guide to Home Caregiving*. Hoboken, N.J.: Wiley, 2001.

Those without families were sometimes confined to hospitals or sanatoriums. People with contagious diseases or disabilities who required constant supervision were also cared for in institutions. Even with family, however, the needs of the elderly or infirm person often exceeded the facilities, time, and energy that the family had to offer. The business of running a household left little time for the family to tend to the needs of the terminally or seriously ill.

Rural areas often made "visiting nurses" available to check on patients who lived far from town and lacked regular transportation for medical visits. These nurses eventually discovered that the needs of the patients went beyond medical care. Patients were grateful for the company of another person in their homes, someone to read their mail to them or run errands. They were grateful not to have to abandon their own homes just because they needed a little assistance from time to time. As the demand for this kind of home care advanced, home attendants found that people needed their services, and the profession of home care aides began to grown.

Advances in modern medicine have made it possible for many illnesses to be treated at home. Hospitals and stores now rent items such as wheelchairs and oxygen tanks, enabling people to have medical equipment available in their own homes. The medical profession is also learning how a person's recovery and treatment can be affected by his or her environment. People generally recover from illnesses better when they are treated in their home environment.

The number of home care agencies has grown from about 1,100 in 1963 to more than 20,000 today.

# THE JOB

Home health care aides enable elderly persons to stay in their own homes. For some clients, just a few visits a week are enough to help them look after themselves. Although physically demanding, the work is often emotionally rewarding. Home care aides may not have access to equipment and facilities such as those found in hospitals, but they also don't have the hospital's frantic pace. Home care aides are expected to take the time to get to know their clients and their individual needs. They perform their duties within the client's home environment, which often is a much better atmosphere than the impersonal rooms of a hospital.

In addition to the elderly, home health care aides assist people of any age who are recovering at home following hospitalization. They also help children whose parents are ill, disabled, or neglectful. Aides may be trained to supply care to people suffering from specific illnesses such as AIDS, Alzheimer's disease, or cancer, or patients with developmental disabilities who lack sufficient daily living skills.

Clients unable to feed themselves may depend on home care aides to shop for food, prepare their meals, feed them, and clean up after meals. Likewise, home health care aides may assist clients in dressing and grooming, including washing, bathing, cleaning teeth and nails, and fixing the clients' hair.

Massages, alcohol rubs, whirlpool baths, and other therapies and treatments may be a part of a client's required care. Home health care aides may work closely with a physician or home nurse in giving medications and dietary supplements and helping with exercises and other therapies. They may check pulses, temperatures, and respiration rates. Occasionally, they may change nonsterile dressings, use special equipment such as a hydraulic lift, or assist with braces or artificial limbs.

Home health care aides working in home care agencies are supervised by a registered nurse, physical therapist, or social worker who assigns them specific duties. Aides report changes in patients' conditions to the supervisor or case manager.

Household chores are often another aspect of the home health care aide's responsibilities. Light housekeeping, such as changing and washing bed linens, doing the laundry and ironing, and dusting, may be necessary. When a home care aide looks after the children of a disabled or neglectful parent, work may include making lunches for the children, helping them with their homework, or providing companionship and adult supervision in the evening.

Personal attention and comfort are important aspects of an aide's care. Home health care aides can provide this support by reading to patients, playing checkers or a computer game, or visiting with an elderly client. Often just listening to a client's personal problems will help the client through the day. Because elderly people do not always have the means to venture out alone, a home health care aide may accompany an ambulatory patient to the park for an afternoon stroll or to the physician's office for an appointment.

# REQUIREMENTS

## High School

Many programs require only a high school diploma for entry-level positions. Previous or additional course work in family and consumer science, cooking, sewing, and meal planning are very helpful, as are courses that focus on family living and home nursing.

## Postsecondary Training

Health care agencies usually focus their training on first aid, hygiene, and the principles of health care. Cooking and nutrition, including meal preparation for patients with specific dietary needs, are often included in the program. Home health care aides may take courses in psychology and child development as well as family living. Because of the need for hands-on work, aides usually learn how to bathe, dress, and feed patients as well as how to help them walk upstairs or get up from bed. The more specific the skill required for certain patients, the more an agency is likely to have more comprehensive instruction.

Most agencies will offer training to prospective employees. Such training may include instruction on how to deal with depressed or reluctant patients, how to prepare easy and nutritious meals, and tips on housekeeping. Specific course work on health and sanitation may also be required.

## Certification or Licensing

Home Care University, a subsidiary of the National Association for Home Care and Hospice, offers the home care aide certification to applications who complete educational and skill requirements and pass a written examination. Contact the association for more information.

The federal government has enacted guidelines for home health aides whose employers receive reimbursement from Medicare. Federal law requires home health aides to pass a competency test covering 12 areas: communication skills; documentation of patient status and care provided; reading and recording vital signs; basic infection control procedures; basic body functions; maintenance of a healthy environment; emergency procedures; physical, emotional, and developmental characteristics of patients; personal hygiene and grooming; safe transfer techniques; normal range of motion and positioning; and basic nutrition.

Federal law suggests at least 75 hours of classroom and practical training supervised by a registered nurse. Training and testing programs may be offered by the employing agency, but they must meet the standards of the Centers for Medicare and Medicaid Services. Training programs vary depending upon state regulations.

### Other Requirements

Caring for people in their own homes can be physically demanding work. Lifting a client for baths and exercise, helping a client up and down stairs, performing housework, and aiding with physical therapy all require that an aide be in good physical condition. Aides do not have the equipment and facilities of a hospital to help them with their work, and this requires adaptability and ingenuity. Oftentimes they must make do with the resources available in a typical home.

An even temperament and a willingness to serve others are important characteristics for home health care aides. People in this occupation should be friendly, patient, sensitive to others' needs, and tactful. At times an aide will have to be stern in dealing with uncooperative patients or calm and understanding with those who are angry, confused, despondent, or in pain. Genuine warmth and respect for others are important attributes. Cheerfulness and a sense of humor can go a long way in establishing a good relationship with a client, and a good relationship can make working with the client much easier.

Home health care aides must be willing to follow instructions and abide by the health plan created for each patient. Aides provide an important outreach service, supporting the care administered by the patient's physician, therapist, or social worker. They are not trained medical personnel, however, and must know the limits of their authority.

## EXPLORING

Home health care aides are employed in many different areas. Interested students can learn more about the work by contacting local agencies and programs that provide home care services and requesting information on the organization's employment guidelines or training programs. Visiting the county or city health department and contacting the personnel director may provide useful information as well. Often, local organizations sponsor open houses to inform the community about the services they provide. This could serve as an excellent opportunity to meet the staff involved in hiring and program development and to learn about job opportunities. In addition, it may be possible to arrange to accompany a home health care aide on a home visit.

## EMPLOYERS

Approximately 921,700 home health care aides are employed in the United States. The primary employers of home health care aides are local social service agencies that provide home care services. Such agencies often have training programs for prospective employees. Home health care aides might also find employment with hospitals that operate their own community outreach programs. Most hospitals, however, hire home health care aides through agencies.

## STARTING OUT

Some social service agencies enlist the aid of volunteers. By contacting agencies and inquiring about such openings, aspiring home care aides can get an introduction to the type of work this profession requires. Also, many agencies or nursing care facilities offer training to prospective employees.

Checking the local Yellow Pages for agencies that provide health care to the aged and disabled or family service organizations can provide a list of employment prospects. Nursing homes, public and private health care facilities, and local chapters of the Red Cross and United Way are likely to hire entry-level employees. The National Association for Home Care and Hospice can also supply information on reputable agencies and departments that employ home care aides.

## ADVANCEMENT

As home health care aides develop their skills and deepen their experience, they may advance to management or supervisory positions. Those who find greater enjoyment working with clients may branch into more specialized care and pursue additional training. Additional experience and education often bring higher pay and increased responsibility.

Aides who wish to work in a clinic or hospital setting may return to school to complete a nursing degree. Other related occupations include social worker, physical or occupational therapist, and dietitian. Along with a desire for advancement, however, must come the willingness to meet additional education and experience requirements.

# EARNINGS

Earnings for home health care aides are comparable to the salaries of nursing and psychiatric aides and nurse assistants. Depending on the agency, considerable flexibility exists in working hours and patient load. For many aides who begin as part-time employees, the starting salary is usually the minimum hourly wage ($7.25 as of this writing). For full-time aides with significant training or experience, earnings may be $8 to $11 per hour. According to the U.S. Department of Labor, median hourly earnings of home health aides were $9.85 in 2009, about $20,450 annually for full-time employment. The most experienced home health care aides earned more than $14.13 an hour (about $29,390 annually for full-time work).

Aides are usually paid only for the time worked in the home. They normally are not paid for travel time between jobs.

Vacation policies and benefits packages vary with the type and size of the employing agency. Many full-time home health care aides receive one week of paid vacation following their first year of employment, and they often receive two weeks of paid vacation each year thereafter. Full-time aides may also be eligible for health insurance and retirement benefits. Some agencies also offer holiday or overtime compensation.

# WORK ENVIRONMENT

Health aides in a hospital or nursing home setting work at a much different pace and in a much different environment than the home health care aide. With home care, aides can take the time to sit with their clients and get to know them. Aides spend a certain amount of time with each client and can perform their responsibilities without the frequent distractions and demands of a hospital. Home surroundings differ from situation to situation. Some homes are neat and pleasant, while others are untidy and depressing. Some patients are angry, abusive, depressed, or otherwise difficult; others are pleasant and cooperative.

Because home health care aides usually have more than one patient, the hours an aide works can fluctuate based on the number of clients and types of services needed. Many clients may be ill or have disabilities. Some may be elderly and have no one else to assist them with light housekeeping or daily errands. These differences can dictate the type of responsibilities a home care aide has for each patient.

Working with the infirm or disabled can be a rewarding experience as aides enhance the quality of their clients' lives with their help and company. However, the personal strains—on the clients as well as the aides—can make the work challenging and occasionally frustrating. There can be difficult emotional demands that aides may find exhausting. Considerable physical activity is involved in this line of work, such as helping patients to walk, dress, or take care of themselves. Traveling from one home to another and running various errands for patients can also be tiring and time-consuming, or it can be a pleasant break.

## OUTLOOK

As government and private agencies develop more programs to assist the dependent, the need for home health care aides will continue to be very strong. Because of the physical and emotional demands of the job, there is high turnover and, therefore, frequent job openings for home health care aides.

Also, the number of people 65 years of age and older is expected to increase substantially, and many of them will require at least some home care. Rising health care costs are causing many insurance companies to consider alternatives to hospital treatment, so many insurance providers now cover home care services. In addition, hospitals and nursing homes are trying to balance the demand for their services and their limitations in staff and physical facilities. The availability of home health care aides can allow such institutions as hospitals and nursing homes to offer quality care to more people. The U.S. Department of Labor projects that employment of home health aides will grow much faster than the average for all occupations through 2018.

## FOR MORE INFORMATION

*For information on caring for the elderly, contact*
**ElderWeb**
1305 Chadwick Drive
Normal, IL 61761
Tel: 309-451-3319
E-mail: info@elderweb.com
http://www.elderweb.com

*For certification information and statistics on the home health care industry, visit the association's Web site.*
**National Association for Home Care and Hospice**
228 Seventh Street, SE
Washington, DC 20003-4306
Tel: 202-547-7424
http://www.nahc.org

# Hospice Workers

## OVERVIEW

*Hospice workers* provide support for terminally ill patients in the final stages of their illness. Hospice care is a benefit under Medicare Hospital Insurance and eligible persons can receive medical and support services for their terminal illnesses. Care is primarily provided in the patients' homes, but may also be provided in nursing homes and hospitals, with the intent to make patients as comfortable and pain-free as medically possible during the final days of their lives. A team of specially trained professionals and volunteers provides hospice care. The National Hospice and Palliative Care Organization estimates that 1.45 million patients are served by hospice organizations each year.

## HISTORY

The hospice concept can be traced to ancient times when shelter and rest (hospitality) were provided for travelers. Home care has also been a tradition in America since the 1880s when public health nurses began traveling to patients' homes to care for the sick and comfort the dying. However, the term *hospice* was first used in 1967 to mean specialized care for dying patients when St. Christopher's Hospice in a residential suburb of London was established. The first hospice in the United States, The Connecticut Hospice, was established in 1974. Today, *hospice* refers to a type of compassionate care and support given to the dying patient and to the patient's family and caregivers. In 2008, there were nearly 4,850 organizations that provided hospice services in the United States.

## QUICK FACTS

**School Subjects**
Health
Psychology

**Personal Skills**
Helping/teaching
Technical/scientific

**Work Environment**
Primarily indoors
Primarily multiple locations

**Minimum Education Level**
Varies according to position

**Salary Range**
Varies according to position

**Certification or Licensing**
Recommended for certain
    positions (certification)
Required for certain
    positions (licensing)

**Outlook**
Faster than the average

**DOT**
N/A

**GOE**
N/A

**NOC**
N/A

**O*NET-SOC**
N/A

# THE JOB

Hospice workers help patients who have a variety of terminal illnesses and who can no longer benefit from curative treatment. Typically, a hospice patient has less than six months to live.

Hospice workers are a team of trained professionals that include administrators, physicians, nurses, counselors, chaplains, therapists, social workers, aides, and volunteers. Hospice organizations rely heavily on volunteers, who must participate in intensive volunteer training. According to a study by the National Hospice and Palliative Care Association of America, in 2008, more than 550,000 hospice volunteers in the United States provided 25 million hours of service.

Hospices use a team approach to plan and coordinate care for the patient. This team includes the patient, family, and the hospice team, all working together. Family or primary caregivers can call for the help of a hospice team member 24 hours a day, seven days a week, and a team member will respond whenever needed.

Hospice workers' job responsibilities are related to their profession. *Hospice medical directors* may be licensed physicians who oversee the medical program and advise the hospice care staff. *Registered nurses* may be responsible for seeing that a member of the hospice team meets the patient's needs. Nurses also visit patients to monitor their emotional and physical symptoms. *Nurse assistants* and *home health care aides* assist the family in the personal care of the patient such as bathing, grooming, and changing the bed linens. *Physical, occupational,* and *speech therapists* help patients with daily living tasks that have become difficult or impossible to perform. *Social workers* help the patient and family deal with the emotions surrounding the illness. They also help locate personal and community resources that may assist the patient or the family. *Volunteer coordinators* organize and direct the volunteer program and for training the volunteer workers. *Chaplains* provide religious support to the patient and family in accordance with their specific religious beliefs. *Music therapists* use music to provide comfort and relaxation to the patient. *Grief therapists* help the family deal with the death of their loved one and cope with their grief.

# REQUIREMENTS

## High School

Persons wishing to obtain a college degree in one of the professions employed by hospice organizations should take a well-balanced college preparatory course in high school, with a good foundation in the

A hospice worker holds the hand of an elderly woman who is terminally ill with congestive heart failure. (*Al Campanie, Syracuse Newspapers/The Image Works*)

sciences. Biology, chemistry, and psychology are important courses. You should take anatomy and physiology if your high school offers these courses. You should also take courses in the humanities and social sciences, as well as classes that improve communication skills.

High school diploma requirements vary with hospice organizations and the volunteer responsibilities. Some volunteer work for example, answering the phones, cleaning, or maintaining grounds, does not require a diploma of any kind. However, a high school diploma would probably be required for any volunteer position that involves patient contact.

## Postsecondary Training

The degree program you should pursue depends on the role you hope to play in the hospice programs. Some positions require a bachelor's degree and others a medical degree or other specialized degree. Many hospitals offer medical rotations in hospice care to physicians, nurses, and other professionals involved in training. Madonna University in Livonia, Michigan, offers the only university-based hospice and palliative studies program of study in the United States. Visit http://www.madonna.edu/pages/hospiceeducation.cfm for more information.

## Certification or Licensing

The certification or licensing requirements are determined by the medical specialty or professional career that you wish to pursue. The hospice itself is usually licensed by the department of health of each state (more than 40 states license hospice programs) and certified by Medicare and Medicaid. Additionally, the National Association for Home Care and Hospice offers certification for home care aides and hospice executives. Contact the association for more information.

## Other Requirements

If you are planning to become involved in hospice care, you should be able to work as a member of a team to provide the support and care that is needed by terminally ill patients and their loved ones and caregivers. You should be compassionate, patient, sensitive, and well organized. Flexibility and the ability to make decisions are important. You should also feel comfortable dealing with the sick and dying.

# EXPLORING

There are many ways to learn more about a career as a hospice worker. You can read books and magazines about hospice care. There are also many Web sites that discuss the career and issues in the field. Visit the Web sites of the professional associations listed at the end of this article. Ask a teacher or counselor to arrange an informational interview with a hospice worker. You also can volunteer to care for a family member who is ill or elderly or volunteer at a local hospice or social services agency.

# EMPLOYERS

Hospice organizations hire hospice workers and also welcome hospice volunteers. As of 2008, there were nearly 4,850 hospice programs in all 50 states, the District of Columbia, and Puerto Rico. About 57 percent of these hospices operated as independent entities, while others were associated with hospitals, home health agencies, and nursing facilities. About 50 percent of hospices are nonprofit organizations.

# STARTING OUT

If you are interested in pursuing a career as a hospice worker, you should consider doing volunteer work at a hospice center, hospital, or nursing home when in high school. This will give you an insight into the hospice environment and its career possibilities.

If you choose to complete professional training, a career services office associated with your degree program may help you locate employment opportunities. In addition, contacts you made in clinical settings while training or volunteering may be helpful. Applying directly to hospices and other health care agencies and answering ads in professional journals can also produce employment opportunities.

## ADVANCEMENT

Advancement opportunities include director and supervisor positions within the hospice program. Other career opportunities may exist with government agencies and organizations associated with hospice and home health care programs. A degree may be required to advance to some positions.

## EARNINGS

Salaries for hospice workers are similar to those of their counterparts in a more typical medical setting and generally are based on the position, the educational requirements for that position, and the level of experience of the worker. According to the *2008–09 Hospice Salary and Benefits Report* conducted by the Hospital and Healthcare Compensation Service in cooperation with the Hospice Association of America, salaries for directors of hospice ranged from $76,005 to $101,944. Salaries for directors of social work and counseling ranged from $54,100 to $72,100, while directors of clinical services earned $67,124 to $85,700.

The Hospital and Healthcare Compensation Service and the Hospice Association of America report the following hourly salary ranges for hospice professionals by job specialty: registered nurse, $24.23 to $28.50; licensed practical nurse, $16.83 to $20.76; physical therapist, $31.62 to $36.50; social worker (with a master's degree in social work), $20.55 to $24.89; and director of volunteer services, $16.37 to $21.84.

Hospice chaplains, music therapists, and grief therapists may earn salaries that range from $20,000 to $40,000 or more annually.

Fringe benefits are usually similar to those of other full-time health care workers and may include sick leave, vacation, health and life insurance, and tuition assistance.

## WORK ENVIRONMENT

Most hospice workers visit terminally ill patients in their homes or in the homes of their caregivers, so the work environment can be as varied as their patients' lifestyles. Some workers are on call 24 hours a day and may be required to travel to homes in all areas of a city or rural area to provide medical and supportive care. Patients and family members can be very tense during this stressful period in their lives, and they may be unpleasant and uncooperative at times. As with any health care profession, hospice workers have the possibility of exposure to contagious diseases; however, proper precautions and training diminish this risk.

## OUTLOOK

Hospice participation has grown at a dramatic rate, especially among those involved with Medicare. According to the National Association for Home Care and Hospice, from 1984 to 2008 the total number of hospices participating in Medicare rose from 31 to 3,346—a nearly 108-fold increase. The number of hospices and patients serviced by them is expected to increase as the population ages and health care costs rise. In addition, families and medical professionals are choosing hospice care because of its holistic, patient-family, in-home-centered philosophy.

## FOR MORE INFORMATION

*For information on hospice care, contact*
**Hospice Education Institute**
3 Unity Square
PO Box 98
Machiasport, ME 04655-0098
Tel: 800-331-1620
E-mail: info@hospiceworld.org
http://www.hospiceworld.org

*For general information about hospice care, contact*
**National Association for Home Care and Hospice**
228 Seventh Street, SE
Washington, DC 20003-4306
Tel: 202-547-7424
http://www.nahc.org

*For industry statistics, contact*
**National Hospice and Palliative Care Organization**
1731 King Street, Suite 100
Alexandria, VA 22314-2720
Tel: 703-837-1500
E-mail: nhpco_info@nhpco.org
http://www.nhpco.org

# Human Services Workers

## OVERVIEW

Under the supervision of social workers, psychologists, sociologists, and other professionals, *human services workers* offer support to families, the elderly, the poor, and others in need. They teach life and communication skills to people in mental health facilities or substance abuse programs. Employed by agencies, shelters, halfway houses, and hospitals, they work individually with clients or in group counseling. They also direct clients to social services and benefits. There are approximately 352,000 human services workers employed in the United States.

## HISTORY

Before the 20th century, charity and philanthropy consisted mainly of donations from the affluent. These donations were distributed by church groups to the needy. No systematic methods were established to follow up on charity cases or improve the conditions of the poor in any permanent way.

After the industrial revolution, public opinion about the inequities of wealth began to change. In 1889, Jane Addams, the daughter of a banker, founded Hull-House in Chicago, an act that is usually considered the birth of formal social work. Addams's philosophy of helping the underprivileged gain a better, more permanent standard of living inspired many others to launch similar programs in other parts of the world. After World War I, social work began to be recognized as a valid career. The Great Depression of the 1930s provided further

## QUICK FACTS

**School Subjects**
Health
Sociology

**Personal Skills**
Communication/ideas
Helping/teaching

**Work Environment**
Primarily indoors
Primarily one location

**Minimum Education Level**
High school diploma

**Salary Range**
$18,300 to $27,940 to $44,760+

**Certification or Licensing**
Recommended (certification)
Required by certain states (licensing)

**Outlook**
Much faster than the average

**DOT**
195

**GOE**
14.07.01

**NOC**
4212

**O*NET-SOC**
21-1093.00

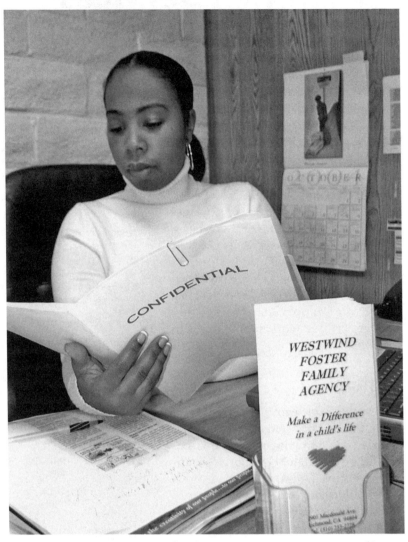

A human services worker at a family services agency reviews case files.
(*Geri Engberg, The Image Works*)

impetus to the growth of social work, as the federal government joined with state, municipal, and private efforts to ease the pain of poverty. The social disruptions of the years following World War II contributed to further growth in social work. Today, social workers and human services workers are employed in a variety of institutional and community settings, administering help and support to the poor, the homeless, the aged, the disabled and mentally ill, substance abusers, parolees, and others having trouble with adjustments in life.

# THE JOB

A group of teenagers in a large high school are concerned about the violence that threatens them every day. They have seen their friends and classmates hurt in the school's hallways, on the basketball court, and in the parking lot. In a place built for their education, they fear for their safety, and each of them has something to say about it. They have something to say to the administration, to the parents, and, most of all, to the kids who carry guns and knives to school. Human services workers come to their aid. Human services workers step in to support the efforts of social workers, psychologists, and other professional agencies or programs. Human services workers may work in a school, a community center, a housing project, or a hospital. They may work as aides, assistants, technicians, or counselors. In the case of the high school students who want to improve conditions in their school, human services workers serve as group leaders under the supervision of a school social worker, meeting with some of the students to discuss their fears and concerns. They also meet with administrators, faculty, and parents. Eventually, they conduct a school-wide series of group discussions—listening, taking notes, offering advice, and most important, empowering people to better their communities and their lives.

The term *human services* covers a wide range of careers, from counseling prison inmates to counseling the families of murder victims; from helping someone with a disability find a job to caring for the child of a teenage mother during the school day. From one-on-one interaction to group interaction, from paperwork to footwork, the human services worker is focused on improving the lives of others. According to the National Organization for Human Services, there are more than 40 occupational titles of human services workers, including adult day care worker, child advocate, crisis intervention counselor, drug abuse counselor, gerontology aide, group activities aide, psychological aide, and social service aide.

As society changes, so do the concerns of human services workers. New societal problems (such as the rapid spread of AIDS among teenagers and the threat of gang violence) require special attention, as do changes in the population (such as the increasing number of elderly people living on their own and the increasing number of minimum-wage workers unable to fully provide for their families). New laws and political movements also affect human services workers because many social service programs rely heavily on federal and state aid. Although government policy makers may be better educated about the issues than the policy makers of years past, social service programs are more threatened than ever before. Despite all these changes in society and the changes in the theories of social work, some things stay the same—human services workers care about the well-being of individuals and communities. They are sensitive to the needs of diverse groups of people, and they are actively involved in meeting the needs of the public.

Human services workers have had many of the same responsibilities throughout the years. They offer their clients counseling, representation, emotional support, and the services they need. Although some human services workers assist professionals with the development and evaluation of social programs, policy analysis, and other administrative duties, most work directly with clients.

This direct work can involve aid to specific populations, such as ethnic groups, women, and the poor. Many human services workers assist poor people in numerous ways. They interview clients to identify needed services. They care for clients' children during job or medical appointments and offer clients emotional support. They determine whether clients are eligible for food stamps, Medicaid, or other welfare programs. In some food stamp programs, aides advise low-income family members how to plan, budget, shop for, and prepare balanced meals, often accompanying or driving clients to the store and offering suggestions on the most nutritious and economical food to purchase.

Some aides serve tenants in public housing projects. They are employed by housing agencies or other groups to help tenants relocate. They inform tenants of the use of facilities and the location of community services, such as recreation centers and clinics. They also explain the management's rules about sanitation and maintenance. They may at times help resolve disagreements between tenants and landlords.

Members of specific populations call on the aid of human services workers for support, information, and representation. The human services worker can provide these clients with counseling and emotional support and direct them to support groups and services. Social workers team with human services workers to reach out to the people; together, they visit individuals, families, and neighborhood groups to publicize the supportive services available.

Other clients of human services workers are those experiencing life-cycle changes. Children, adolescents, and the elderly may require assistance in making transitions. Human services workers help parents find proper day care for their children. They educate young mothers about how to care for an infant. They counsel children struggling with family problems or peer pressure. They offer emo-

## Median Annual Earnings for Social and Human Service Assistants by Employer, 2009

Federal executive branch: $42,740

State government: $35,810

Local government: $34,130

Individual and family services: $28,340

Vocational rehabilitation services: $26,110

Residential mental retardation, mental health, and substance abuse facilities: $24,770

Source: U.S. Department of Labor

tional support to gay, lesbian, and bisexual teenagers and involve them in support groups. Some programs help the elderly stay active and help them prepare meals and clean their homes. They also assist the elderly in getting to and from hospitals and community centers and stay in touch with these clients through home visits and telephone calls.

Some human services workers focus on specific problems, such as drug and alcohol abuse. Human services workers assist in developing, organizing, and conducting programs dealing with the causes of and remedies for substance abuse. Workers may help individuals trying to overcome drug or alcohol addiction to master practical skills, such as cooking and doing laundry, and teach them ways to communicate more effectively with others. Domestic violence is also a problem receiving more attention, as more and more people leave abusive situations. Shelters for victims require counselors, assistants, tutors, and day care personnel for their children. Human services workers may also teach living and communication skills in homeless shelters and mental health facilities.

Record keeping is an important part of the duties of human services workers, because records may affect a client's eligibility for future benefits, the proper assessment of a program's success, and the prospect of future funding. Workers prepare and maintain records and case files of every person with whom they work.

They record clients' responses to the various programs and treatment. They must also track costs in group homes in order to stay within budget.

# REQUIREMENTS

## High School

Some employers hire people with only a high school education, but these employees might find it hard to move beyond clerical positions. Interested high school students should plan to attend a college or university and should take classes in English, mathematics, political science, psychology, and sociology.

## Postsecondary Training

Certificate and associate's degree programs in human services, gerontology, or one of the social or behavioral sciences are offered at community and junior colleges, vocational-technical institutes, and other postsecondary institutions. It is also possible to pursue a bachelor's degree in human services or a related field, such as social work, counseling, or rehabilitation. Almost 500 human services education programs exist; academic programs such as these prepare students for occupations in the human services. Because the educators at these colleges and universities stay in regular contact with the social work employers in their area, the programs are continually revised to meet the changing needs of the field. Students are exposed early and often to the kinds of situations they may encounter on the job.

Undergraduate and graduate programs typically include courses in psychology, sociology, crisis intervention, family dynamics, therapeutic interviewing, rehabilitation, and gerontology.

## Certification or Licensing

The National Organization for Human Services, in collaboration with the Council for Standards in Human Services Education and the Center for Credentialing and Education (CCE), offers the human services board certified practitioner designation to applicants who meet educational requirements and pass an examination. Contact the CCE (http://www.cce-global.org) for more information.

Some states may require certain types of human services workers to be licensed. Contact your state's department of licensing for more information about requirements in your state.

## Other Requirements

Many people perform human services work because they want to make a difference in their community. They may also like connecting on a personal level with other people, offering them emotional support, helping them sort out problems, and teaching them how to care for themselves and their families. A genuine interest in the lives and concerns of others and a sensitivity to their situations are important to a human services worker. An artistic background can also be valuable in human services. Some programs in mental health facilities, domestic violence shelters, and other group homes use art therapy. Painting, music, dance, and creative writing are sometimes incorporated into counseling sessions, providing a client with alternative modes of expression.

In addition to the rewarding aspects of the job, a human services worker must be prepared to take on difficult responsibilities. The work can be very stressful. The problems of some populations—such as prison inmates, battered women and children, substance abusers, and the poor—can seem insurmountable. Their stories and day-to-day lives can seem tragic. Even if human services workers are not counseling clients, they are working directly with clients on some level. Just helping a person fill out an application or prepare a household budget requires a good disposition and the ability to be supportive. Clients may not welcome help and may not even care about their own well-being. In these cases, a human services worker must remain firm but supportive and encouraging. Patience is very important, whatever the area of human service.

The workload for a human services worker can also be overwhelming. An agency with limited funding cannot always afford to hire the number of employees it needs. A human services worker employed by an understaffed agency will probably be overworked. This can sometimes result in employee burnout.

## EXPLORING

To get an idea of the requirements of human service, you can volunteer your time to a local human services agency or institution. Religious organizations also involve young people in volunteer work, as do the Red Cross, the Boy Scouts, and the Girl Scouts. Volunteer work could include reading to blind or elderly people and visiting nursing homes and halfway homes. You might get involved organizing group recreation programs at the YMCA or YWCA or performing light clerical duties in an office. You could also encourage any high school organizations to which you belong to become actively involved in charity work.

Some members of high school organizations also perform social services within their own schools, educating classmates on the dangers of gangs, unsafe sex, and substance abuse. By being actively involved in your community, you can gain experience in human services as well as build up a history of volunteer service that will impress future employers.

## EMPLOYERS

Approximately 352,000 human services workers are employed in the United States. Sixty-five percent work in the health care and social assistance industries. Nearly 24 percent are employed by local and state governments. Employment settings include agency offices, community centers, group homes, halfway houses, mental health facilities, hospitals, shelters, and the private homes of clients.

## STARTING OUT

Students may find jobs through their counselors, career services office, or local and state human services agencies. Sometimes summer jobs and volunteer work can develop into full-time employment upon graduation. Employers try to be selective in their hiring because many human services jobs involve direct contact with people who are impaired and therefore vulnerable to exploitation. Experience with helping others is a definite advantage.

## ADVANCEMENT

Job performance has some bearing on pay raises and advancement for human services workers. However, career advancement almost always depends on formal education, such as a bachelor's or master's degree in social work, counseling, rehabilitation, or some other related field. Many employers encourage their workers to further their education and some may even reimburse part of the costs of school. In addition, many employers provide in-service training such as seminars and workshops.

## EARNINGS

Salaries of human services workers depend in part on their employer and amount of experience. According to the U.S. Department of Labor, median annual earnings of social and human service assistants were $27,940 in 2009. Salaries ranged from less than $18,300 to more than $44,760.

Benefits for full-time workers include vacation and sick time, health, and sometimes dental, insurance, and pension or 401(k) plans.

## WORK ENVIRONMENT

Most human services workers work a standard 40-hour week, spending time both in the office and in the field interviewing clients and performing other support services. Some weekend and evening work may be required, but compensatory time off is usually granted. Workers in residential settings generally work in shifts. Because group homes need 24-hour staffing, workers usually work some evenings and weekends.

Work conditions are affected by the size and location of the town in which the work is found. The societal problems of large, urban areas are different from those of small, rural areas. In a city, human services workers deal with issues of crime, racism, gang warfare, and violence in the schools. These problems can exist in smaller communities as well, but human services workers in rural areas focus more on work with the elderly and the poor. Rural communities typically have an older population, with people living deeper in the country and farther from public and private services. This can require more transportation time. The social services in rural areas, because of lower salaries and poorer facilities, typically have trouble attracting workers.

Offices and facilities may be clean and cheerful, or they may be dismal, cramped, and inadequately equipped. While out in the field with clients, workers may also find themselves in dangerous, squalid areas. In a large city, workers can rely on public transportation, whereas workers in a rural community must often drive long distances.

## OUTLOOK

Employment for human services workers will grow much faster than the average for all occupations through 2018, according to the U.S. Department of Labor. The best opportunities will be in private social service agencies as more state and local governments contract out services. Employment will be strong in mental health counseling, substance abuse treatment, job-training programs, residential care facilities, adult day care, meal delivery programs, and support for individuals during medical emergencies. Correctional facilities are also expected to employ many more human services workers. Because counseling inmates and offenders can be undesirable work, there are a number of high-paying jobs available in that area.

New ideas in treating people with disabilities or mental illness also influence employment growth in group homes and residential care facilities. Public concern for the homeless—many of whom are former mental patients who were released under service reductions—as well as for troubled teenagers, and those with substance abuse problems, is likely to bring about new community-based programs and group residences.

Job prospects in public agencies are not as bright as they once were because of fiscal policies that tighten eligibility requirements for federal welfare and other payments. State and local governments are expected to remain major employers, however, as the burden of providing social services such as welfare, child support, and nutrition programs is shifted from the federal government to the state and local level. In larger cities, such as New York or Washington, D.C., jobs in the public sector will be more plentiful than in smaller cities because of the higher demand. There is also a higher burnout rate in the larger cities, resulting in more job opportunities as people vacate their positions for other careers.

## FOR MORE INFORMATION

*For more information on careers in counseling, contact*
**American Counseling Association**
5999 Stevenson Avenue
Alexandria, VA 22304-3304
Tel: 800-347-6647
http://www.counseling.org

*To access the online publication* Choices: Careers in Social Work, *visit the association's Web site.*
**National Association of Social Workers**
750 First Street, NE, Suite 700
Washington, DC 20002-4241
http://www.socialworkers.org

*For information on certification, contact*
**National Organization for Human Services**
5341 Old Highway 5, Suite 206, #214
Woodstock, GA 30188-2494
Tel: 770-924-8899
E-mail: admin@nationalhumanservices.org
http://www.nationalhumanservices.org

*For information about employment with government human service agencies, contact*
**U.S. Department of Health and Human Services**
200 Independence Avenue, SW
Washington, DC 20201-0004
Tel: 877-696-6775
http://www.hhs.gov

*The following is a job search Web site for social services and social work positions:*

**SocialService.Com**
http://www.socialservice.com

# Nonprofit Social Service Directors

## OVERVIEW

*Nonprofit social service directors,* also known as *nonprofit directors, nonprofit chief executive officers, nonprofit administrators,* or *social and community service managers,* are at the top rung on the agency's ladder. No matter what area the agency specializes in—health care, services for the aging, or youth development, for example—the director is the individual who spearheads the organization's efforts, operations, and progress. A director's duties may include hiring and managing staff, fund-raising, budgeting, public relations, and, depending on the agency, working directly with the clientele served.

## HISTORY

Social service organizations have been around in various forms for hundreds of years. During the Middle Ages, organizations formed to care for the sick and the poor. By the 1800s, the industrial revolution was changing society's structure as numerous people moved from small towns and farms to cities where they worked in industries and had few, if any, established social support systems. The cities became more crowded, wages were low, and life became more complicated. After the Civil War, there was an explosion of social service organizations—groups caring for the sick and the poor, and, increasingly, for immigrants. Under President Roosevelt's administration during the 1930s, many New Deal programs, such as unemployment insurance, were established to help people deal with the effects of the Great Depression. During the 1960s, President Johnson's administration followed a similar agenda of promoting the well-being of all citizens with the "Great Society" programs, such as Medicare. These programs increased the role of the government in the welfare of individuals and stimulated the growth of private social service organizations. In the years that followed, the older organizations expanded and many new organizations emerged.

By the end of the 20th century, however, social support systems had begun to change. The federal government, responding to the unpopularity of the expense of many government social service programs, eliminated some programs and cut back on many others. Perhaps the best-known cutback was the Welfare Reform Bill, which was designed to shorten the length of time welfare recipients receive benefits. Reforms at the national level mean that state governments often find themselves trying to provide money to keep programs running. If the funds can't be found at the state level, the slack may be picked up at the city level. If the city is unable to come up with the necessary funds, the services usually pass out of the hands of governmental officials altogether and into the hands of local or national nonprofit organizations.

The need for nongovernmental organizations to fill in gaps left by federal, state, and local programs has changed the profile of charity work. Whereas many organizations once had untrained volunteers, they now often require trained, full-time staff. As nonprofit social service work has become more crucial to the national infrastructure, nonprofits have become increasingly professional. Nonprofit organizations are dependent on intelligent, educated, and savvy direction in order to work. Fund-raising, budgeting, resource management, and public relations are just a few areas where top-notch business skills are a necessity. The role of those who run the organizations—administrators, executive directors, and directors—is crucial.

## THE JOB

Anyone looking for a career that provides a diversity of responsibilities, satisfaction, meaning, action, and a wide realm of options should certainly consider entering the field of social work. Social workers are people who are committed to making a positive difference in the human condition, and the director of an organization has the primary responsibility of seeing that the organization achieves its goals and positively affects the lives of the people it is designed to serve.

An aspect of social work that sets it apart from other helping professions is the concept of helping people in their environments. Social workers help clients not only with how they feel about a situation, but also with what they can do about it. For example, a woman suffering stress from being a single parent may be referred by a social worker to a child care agency. The social worker also might help her explore other options, such as getting flextime at work. In addition, the social worker might provide therapy or counseling or refer the client to a qualified therapist for assistance in managing her stress. A wide variety of nonprofit organizations are at work in the United States today, and each has a different mission and set of services.

Because it now takes such a high level of professional sophistication to keep a nonprofit going, directing these sorts of organizations is becoming a complex, challenging, and varied career. At one time, the biggest prerequisite for those who wanted to work in social services was a big heart. Today, compassion is still a necessary quality to have, but knowledge, skill, and talent are just as important. A director of a social services organization may be in charge of managing staff, overseeing the budget, spearheading fund-raising efforts, and handling public relations issues.

Sheri Flanigan served for three years as the executive director of La Casa Latina Inc., a nonprofit organization with the mission to "empower the Latino population to become part of the Siouxland [Sioux City, Iowa] community." Flanigan says about her work, "There was no 'typical day.' I spent about half of my time on administration: budgeting, fund-raising, grant writing, staff supervision, community meetings, and board meetings. Because we were small (five staff members and a $150,000 budget), I did all of the bookkeeping and payroll. The other half of my time, I provided direct services—translations and interpretation primarily. I also filled in when another staff member was out."

Flanigan notes that the diversity of her experiences was one of the best parts of the job. Because she worked for a small organization, she could work on both a macro and a micro level. She was able to see the fruits of her organization's labors on a community-wide level, but she also enjoyed the time she was able to spend working directly with the agency's clients.

In any nonprofit organization, even as the top individual in the structure, the nature of a director's work likely will be determined largely by a board of directors. This board, plus the size and nature of the organization, will define the director's duties to a large extent.

# REQUIREMENTS

## High School

If you're interested in nonprofit social services work, you'll want to concentrate on humanities and social science courses such as English, history, government, sociology, and psychology. Such courses will give you perspective on the issues confronting the people that a nonprofit organization will be trying to help. Communication skills are critical, so in addition to English, take public speaking courses to hone your skills. The ability to speak a foreign language will be a big plus in many organizations; consider taking Spanish, as it is the second most common language spoken in the United States. At the director level of a nonprofit agency, you will be responsible for budget expenditures; therefore, you should have mathematics and accounting knowledge, so be sure to include these classes in your schedule. Finally, take computer science courses so that you will be able to use the computer for activities such as creating budgets, writing grant proposals, and keeping a database of information on clients.

## Postsecondary Training

Most nonprofit social service organizations will require that you have a degree in social work from a college or university program accredited by the Council on Social Work Education. The undergraduate degree is the bachelor of social work (B.S.W.). Graduate degrees include the master of social work (M.S.W.) and the doctorate in social work (D.S.W.) or Ph.D. The undergraduate degree will allow you to find entry-level positions at many agencies. Typical courses of study for the B.S.W. include classes in social welfare policies, human behavior and the social environment, research methods, and ethics. In addition, accredited programs require you to complete at least 400 hours of supervised field experience. To advance to the level of director, you will need to have a master's or doctorate degree. Obtaining an M.S.W. degree usually requires two years of courses along with 900 hours of supervised fieldwork. You may be able to enter a master's program without having a B.S.W.; however, you should have a background that includes psychology, sociology, biology, economics, and social work courses.

## Certification or Licensing

According to the U.S. Department of Labor, all states have some type of licensing, certification, or registration requirement for those practicing social work and using professional titles. However, the standards and requirements vary from state to state, and those wanting to work as social workers will need to check with their state licensing boards. These licensing, certification, or registration requirements may or may not be necessary for the director, depending on the nature of the organization and the duties of the director. Again, those wanting to work as directors will need to contact the regulatory board of the state in which they want to work to find out specific requirements. The Association of Social Work Boards may also be able to provide such information (see the end of this article for contact information).

### Other Requirements

It takes a certain kind of person to succeed in social services. According to Sheri Flanigan, "You can't be afraid to 'touch' low-income people. From my experiences, I find that even the most well-meaning people have difficulty working in this field if they are uncomfortable interacting with the clientele. In addition, social services are notoriously understaffed, so you also have to be willing to do the work (answer the phone, make copies, etc.). Even though you shouldn't be doing these things for a large portion of the day as a director, you have to be willing to work side by side with the other staff." Social services workers and directors also need to be emotionally stable, objective about situations they face, and responsible.

## EXPLORING

The best way of exploring this field is by doing volunteer work for a nonprofit social service organization such as a hospice, shelter, or community outreach organization. Volunteering will give you exposure to the work environment as well as the situations an organization's clients face and help you develop your listening and communications skills. It can also give you an understanding of the way nonprofits work and the kind of expectations employers will have.

Sheri Flanigan agrees and says, "Volunteer at a variety of social service organizations. This will give you the opportunity to see close-up how these types of organizations function and to evaluate the pros and the cons. The experience will also look good on a resume."

## EMPLOYERS

Nonprofit social service organizations vary in size, purpose, and location. There are large, national nonprofit youth advocacy agencies in the thick of policy issues in Washington, D.C., for example. On the other hand, there are hospices, shelters, and youth support centers in small, community-oriented settings. The nature of the work a director does may also vary, depending on the organization and its size, needs, goals, and board of directors. For example, some social welfare nonprofits focus on changing legislation or public perceptions of certain social issues. These organizations will work differently from those that focus more on working directly with those needing services.

## STARTING OUT

With your B.S.W. or M.S.W. in hand, you should be able to find entry-level work in the social services field. Your college career services office will have contacts to get you started, and the contacts you've made through your professors and colleagues will be invaluable in referring you to vacant positions.

Many social service directors started their careers as volunteers, then, as employees, they worked their way up the ranks. Sheri Flanigan entered the field as a Volunteers in Service to America (VISTA) worker. "VISTA was an excellent way for me to become familiar with the social service organization without having to start at entry level. I believe that service corps is what you make of it. It is easy as a volunteer not to put a lot of effort into the job, but don't fall into that trap. It is an excellent time to explore your opportunities, and to put a lot of effort into making your project work."

## ADVANCEMENT

As the director or executive director of an organization, it can be difficult to see advancement opportunities because these people are already at the top levels of their organizations. A director, however, may see advancement as broadening the goals of his or her organization, increasing funding, or raising public awareness about the issues the organization addresses. Directors can also advance by moving from one nonprofit to another, larger nonprofit agency. Sheri Flanigan has a recommendation: "Look to grow your organization. You start as the executive director of a small nonprofit organization and soon you're the executive director of a large nonprofit—an organization that you nurtured and grew. There is also the possibility of being hired at a larger organization or an organization more tailored to your interests."

## EARNINGS

Salaries in nonprofit work are typically lower than those paid for comparable work in the for-profit sector. In addition, salaries in the nonprofit sector vary tremendously depending on the size, location, and purpose of the organization. Large, high-profile nonprofits with specialized staff and budgets in the millions of dollars, for example, may pay directors well over $100,000, but six-figure salaries are still the exception in this field. The U.S. Department of Labor reports that salaries for social and community service managers, a career similar to that of nonprofit social services directors, ranged from less than $33,440 to more than $96,330, with a median salary of $56,600 in 2009. According to Salary.com, the median annual income in December 2009 for social service directors was approximately $92,300. The lowest paid directors earned less than $68,907 and highest paid directors earned $117,116 or more.

The business publication *The NonProfit Times,* which conducts periodic salary surveys, reports that the average earnings for CEOs and executive directors at nonprofit social services and welfare organizations were approximately $100,118 in 2006. In addition to information on CEOs' pay, the survey also included earnings information for other top administrative positions. The survey showed the national average for development directors was $65,004; for program directors, $60,577; and for directors of volunteers, $38,423. Additionally, the survey reported that salaries varied depending on a specific organization's budget. The median salaries for executive directors of nonprofit organizations with annual budgets of $500,000 or less were $56,500, while the median salaries of executive directors of nonprofits with budgets of $1 million to $9.9 million were $90,413. Directors working for nonprofit organizations with budgets of $50 million or more reported average salaries of $207,145. It is important to keep in mind that the top director job is an advanced position. Those just starting out in the field will earn much less than CEOs. People in this field, however, find that they have the reward of emotional satisfaction not found in every job.

Nonprofit organizations often offer benefits packages that can't be beat. In most agencies, employees can expect liberal annual paid vacation days, generous sick leave, health and hospitalization insurance, retirement plans, and good personnel practices.

## WORK ENVIRONMENT

Nonprofits make great employers because of the positive work environment that they promote; nonprofits are typically humanitarian, responsive to stress, and supportive emotionally. However, these organizations almost always are run on tight budgets, and directors may have to deal with the constant threat of cutbacks or even closure. This can be stressful, and the director must concentrate on the "business" aspect of the work by getting funding, keeping costs down, and meeting with legislators or potential donors. Directors interact with many different people throughout their workdays and must be able to handle a variety of social situations. The tone of the work environment—dedicated, creative, community oriented—is often set by the director's actions. Working hard and long hours promotes commitment to the job by everyone.

## OUTLOOK

According to the U.S. Department of Labor, numerous job opportunities will be available in social services through 2018. Overall employment in the social services industry is projected to grow much faster than the average for all occupations. The expected rapid growth is due to expanding services for the elderly, the mentally and physically disabled, and families in crisis. The elderly comprise a rapidly expanding segment of the population that is likely to need a wide range of social services. The growing emphasis on providing home care services, enabling aging seniors to remain at home rather than relocate to costly skilled nursing facilities, will contribute to employment growth in the social services industry. A continuing influx of foreign-born nationals to the United States will spur the demand for a range of social services, such as financial, relocation, and job training assistance. Child protective services and special groups, such as adults who were abused as children, are also on the rise. In addition, crime, juvenile delinquency, mental illness, developmental disabilities, HIV/AIDS, and individual and family crises will spur demand for social services. Every agency will need to be overseen by a capable and savvy director. Many job openings will also stem from the need to replace nonprofit social service directors who leave their positions.

## FOR MORE INFORMATION

*This alliance of colleges, universities, and nonprofit organizations prepares undergraduates for careers with youth and human services agencies. For more information, contact*
American Humanics
1100 Walnut Street, Suite 1900
Kansas City, MO 64106-2239
Tel: 816-561-6415
http://www.humanics.org

*For information on volunteer opportunities, visit*
**Americorps VISTA (Volunteers In Service To America)**
http://www.americorps.gov/about/programs/vista.asp

*For a list of regulatory agencies or for a comparison of state regulations regarding licensing, certification, and registration, contact*
**Association of Social Work Boards**
400 South Ridge Parkway, Suite B
Culpeper, VA 22701-3791
Tel: 800-225-6880
http://www.aswb.org

*For information on social work careers and educational programs, contact*
**Council on Social Work Education**
1725 Duke Street, Suite 200
Alexandria, VA 22314-3457
Tel: 703-683-8080
E-mail: info@cswe.org
http://www.cswe.org

*For more information on nonprofits, contact*
**Independent Sector**
1602 L Street, NW, Suite 900
Washington, DC 20036-5682
Tel: 202-467-6100
E-mail: info@independentsector.org
http://independentsector.org

*To access the online publication* Choices: Careers in Social Work, *check out the association's Web site.*
**National Association of Social Workers**
750 First Street, NE, Suite 700
Washington, DC 20002-4241
Tel: 202-408-8600
http://www.naswdc.org

*For information on certification, contact*
**National Organization for Human Services**
5341 Old Highway 5, Suite 206, #214
Woodstock, GA 30188-2494
Tel: 770-924-8899
E-mail: admin@nationalhumanservices.org
http://www.nationalhumanservices.org

# Occupational Therapists

## OVERVIEW

*Occupational therapists (OTs)* select and direct therapeutic activities designed to develop or restore maximum function to individuals with disabilities. There are approximately 104,500 occupational therapists employed in the United States.

## HISTORY

Since about the 14th century, physicians have recognized the therapeutic value of providing activities and occupations for their patients. Observations that mental patients tended to recover more quickly from their illnesses if provided with tasks and duties led physicians to involve their patients in such activities as agriculture, weaving, working with animals, and sewing. Over time, this practice became quite common, and the conditions of many patients were improved.

Occupational therapy as we know it today had its beginning after World War I. The need to help disabled veterans of that war, and years later the veterans of World War II, stimulated the growth of this field. Even though its inception was in the psychiatric field, occupational therapy has developed an equally important role in other medical fields, including rehabilitation of physically disabled patients.

Traditionally, occupational therapists taught creative arts such as weaving, clay modeling, leatherwork, jewelry making, and other crafts to promote their patients' functional skills. Today, occupational therapists focus more on providing activities that are designed

## QUICK FACTS

**School Subjects**
Biology
Health

**Personal Skills**
Helping/teaching
Mechanical/manipulative

**Work Environment**
Primarily indoors
Primarily one location

**Minimum Education Level**
Master's degree

**Salary Range**
$45,340 to $69,630 to
$100,430+

**Certification or Licensing**
Required

**Outlook**
Much faster than the average

**DOT**
076

**GOE**
14.06.01

**NOC**
3143

**O\*NET-SOC**
29-1122.00

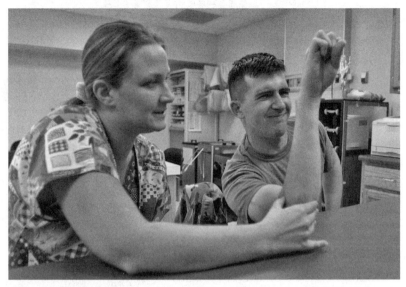

An occupational therapist helps a soldier stretch arm muscles he injured when he fell through a floor during a house raid in Iraq. (*Christopher Berkey, AP Photo*)

to promote skills needed in daily living, including self-care; employment education and job skills, such as typing, the operation of computers and computer programs, or the use of power tools; and community and social skills.

It is important to note the difference between occupational therapists and physical therapists. Physical therapy is chiefly concerned with helping people with physical disabilities or injuries to regain functions, or adapt to or overcome their physical limitations. Occupational therapists work with physical factors but also the psychological and social elements of their clients' disabilities, helping them become as independent as possible in the home, school, and workplace. Occupational therapists work not only with the physically challenged, but with people who have mental and emotional disabilities as well.

## THE JOB

Occupational therapists use a wide variety of activities to help clients attain their goals for productive, independent living. These goals include developing maximum self-sufficiency in activities of daily living, such as eating, dressing, writing, using a telephone and other communication resources, as well as functioning in the community and the workplace.

In developing a therapeutic program for a client, the occupational therapist often works as a member of a team that can include physicians, nurses, psychiatrists, physical therapists, speech therapists, rehabilitation counselors, social workers, and other specialists. OTs use creative, educational, and recreational activities, as well as human ingenuity, in helping people achieve their full potential, regardless of their disabilities. Each therapy program is designed specifically for the individual client.

Occupational therapists help clients explore their likes and dislikes, their abilities, and their creative, educational, and recreational experiences. Therapists help people choose activities that have the most appeal and value for them. For example, an activity may be designed to promote greater dexterity for someone with arthritic fingers. Learning to use an adapted computer might help a young person with a spinal cord injury to succeed in school and career goals. The therapist works with the clients' interests and helps them develop practical skills and functional independence.

The occupational therapist may work with a wide range of clients. They may assist a client in learning to use an artificial limb. Another client may have suffered a stroke or other neurological disability, and the therapist works with the client to redevelop the client's motor functions or re-educate his or her muscle function. Therapists may assist in the growth and development of premature infants, or they may work with disabled children, helping them learn motor skills or develop skills and tools that will aid them in their education and social interaction.

Some therapists also conduct research to develop new types of therapies and activities and to measure the effectiveness of a therapy program. They may also design and make special equipment or splints to help clients perform their activities.

Other duties may include supervision of volunteer workers, student therapists, and occupational therapy assistants who give instruction in a particular skill. Therapists must prepare reports to keep members of the professional team informed.

*Chief occupational therapists* in a hospital may teach medical and nursing students the principles of occupational therapy. Many occupational therapists have administrative duties such as directing different kinds of occupational therapy programs, coordinating patient activities, and acting as consultants or advisors to local and state health departments, mental health authorities, and the division of vocational rehabilitation.

# REQUIREMENTS

## High School

Since you will need to get a college degree, taking college preparatory classes in high school is a must. Courses such as biology, chemistry, and health will expose you to the science fields. Other courses, such as art and social sciences, will help give you an understanding of other aspects of your future work. Also important is a strong background in English. Remember, occupational therapy is a career oriented toward helping people. To be able to work with many different people with different needs, you will need excellent communication skills. Also keep in mind that college admission officers will look favorably at any experience you have had working in the health care field, either in volunteer or paid positions.

## Postsecondary Training

As an undergraduate, you should take courses that emphasize the biological and behavioral sciences. Your studies should include classes on anatomy, physiology, neurology, psychology, human growth and development, and sociology.

Anyone wishing to receive the professional credential, occupational therapist, registered (OTR), from the National Board for Certification in Occupational Therapy (NBCOT) must have completed at least a master's degree in the field. Graduate programs are accredited by the Accreditation Council for Occupational Therapy Education, which is a part of the American Occupational Therapy Association (AOTA). Visit http://www.aota.org/Students/Schools.aspx for a list of accredited programs.

The AOTA recommends that students interested in pursuing graduate study in occupational therapy first earn bachelor's degrees in biology, kinesiology, psychology, sociology, anthropology, liberal arts, or anatomy.

Graduate occupational therapy programs cover general medical and surgical conditions and interpretation of the principles and practice of occupational therapy in pediatrics, psychiatry, orthopedics, general medicine, and surgery. In addition, emphasis is put on research and critical thinking. Management and administration are also covered in graduate programs.

In addition to classroom work, you must complete fieldwork requirements. According to the AOTA, students need to complete the equivalent of 24 weeks of supervised experience working with clients. This may be done on a full-time basis or a part-time (but not less than half-time) schedule. This training must be completed in order to qualify for professional certification.

In addition to these full-time study options, there are a limited number of part-time and evening programs that allow prospective occupational therapists to work in another field while completing their requirements in occupational therapy.

## Certification or Licensing

All states and the District of Columbia regulate the practice of occupational therapy through certification and licensing. National certification is granted by the NBCOT. In order to take the NBCOT exam, you must graduate from an accredited program and complete the clinical practice period. Those who pass this written test are given the designation of occupational therapist, registered, and may use the initials OTR after their names. Initial certification is good for five years and must be renewed every five years after that. Many hospitals and other employers require that their occupational therapists have the OTR designation. In addition, the NBCOT offers several specialty certifications, including board certification in gerontology, mental health, pediatrics, and physical rehabilitation, and specialty certification in driving and community mobility; environmental modification; feeding, eating, and swallowing; and low vision. To receive a specialty certification, you must fulfill education and experience requirements as well as pass an exam.

Licensing (or other forms of professional regulation) is required by all states. License requirements generally include graduation from an accredited program, passing the NBCOT certification exam, payment of license fees, and, in some cases, passing an exam covering state statutes and regulations. License renewal requirements vary by state.

## Other Requirements

In order to succeed as an occupational therapist, you should enjoy working with people. You should have a patient, calm, and compassionate temperament and have the ability to encourage and inspire your clients. Like your clients, you may encounter frustrating situations as a therapist. For example, it can be difficult and stressful when a client does not respond to treatment as you had hoped. In such situations, occupational therapists need to be persistent, not giving up on the client. Imagination and creativity are also important at such times, because you may need to think of new ways to address the client's problem and create new methods or tools for the client to use.

# EXPLORING

While in high school, you should meet with occupational therapists, visit the facilities where they work, and gain an understanding of the types of equipment and skills they use. Many hospitals and occupational therapy facilities and departments also have volunteer opportunities, which will give you strong insight into this career.

## EMPLOYERS

There are approximately 104,500 occupational therapists at work in ambulatory health care services, hospitals, schools, nursing homes, home health agencies, mental health centers, adult day care programs, outpatient clinics, and residential care facilities. A small number of therapists are self-employed, in either solo or group practice or in consulting firms. Approximately 31 percent of occupational therapists work part time.

## STARTING OUT

Your school's career services office is usually the best place to start your job search as a newly graduated occupational therapist. You may also apply directly to government agencies (such as the U.S. Public Health Service), private hospitals, and clinics. In addition, the AOTA can provide job seekers with assistance at its Web site, http://aota.otjoblink.org.

## ADVANCEMENT

Newly graduated occupational therapists usually begin as staff therapists and may qualify as senior therapists after several years on the job. The U.S. Army, Navy, Air Force, Coast Guard, and the U.S. Public Health Service commission occupational therapists; other branches of the federal service give civil service ratings. Experienced therapists may become directors of occupational therapy programs in large hospitals, clinics, or workshops, or they may become teachers. Some positions are available as program coordinators and as consultants with large institutions and agencies.

A few colleges and health agencies offer advanced courses in the treatment of special disabilities, such as those resulting from cerebral palsy. Some institutions provide in-service programs for therapists.

## EARNINGS

According to the U.S. Department of Labor, median salaries for occupational therapists were $69,630 in 2009. The lowest paid 10 percent earned $45,340 or less a year, and the top paid 10 percent earned more than $100,430. The AOTA reports that its members earned median annual salaries of $55,800 in 2006.

Salaries for occupational therapists often vary according to where they work. In areas where the cost of living is higher, occupational therapists generally receive higher pay. Occupational therapists employed in public schools earn salaries that vary by school district. In some states, they are classified as teachers and are paid accordingly.

Therapists employed at hospitals and government and public agencies generally receive full benefit packages that include vacation and sick pay, health insurance, and retirement benefits. Self-employed therapists and those who run their own businesses must provide their own benefits.

## WORK ENVIRONMENT

Occupational therapists work in occupational therapy workshops or clinics. As mentioned earlier, these workshops or clinics can be found at a variety of locations, such as hospitals, long-term care facilities, schools, and adult day care centers. No matter what the location, though, these workshops and clinics are well-lighted, pleasant settings. Generally, therapists work eight-hour days and 40-hour weeks, with some evening work required in a few organizations.

## OUTLOOK

Opportunities for occupational therapists are expected to be highly favorable through 2018 and will grow much faster than the average for all careers, according to the *Occupational Outlook Handbook*. This growth will occur as a result of the increasing number of middle-aged and elderly people who require therapeutic services. Acute hospital, orthopedic, and rehabilitation settings will provide strong employment opportunities since the elderly are often treated in these places. Additionally, the U.S. Department of Labor reports that driver rehabilitation, ergonomic consulting, and fall-prevention training for the elderly are practice areas that are growing in popularity.

The demand for occupational therapists is also increasing because of growing public interest in and government support for people with disabilities and for occupational therapy programs helping people attain the fullest possible functional status. The demand for rehabilitative and long-term care services is expected to grow strongly over the next decade. There will be numerous opportunities for work with mental health clients, children, and the elderly, as well as with those with disabling conditions.

As the health care industry continues to be restructured, there should be many more opportunities for occupational therapists in nontraditional settings, including schools. This factor and proposed changes in the laws should create an excellent climate for therapists wishing to enter private practice. Home health care will experience strong growth in the next decade.

## FOR MORE INFORMATION

*Visit the association's Web site to find out about accredited occupational therapy programs, career information, and news related to the field.*

American Occupational Therapy Association
4720 Montgomery Lane
PO Box 31220
Bethesda, MD 20824-1220
Tel: 301-652-2682
http://www.aota.org

*For information on certification requirements, contact*
National Board for Certification in Occupational Therapy
12 South Summit Avenue, Suite 100
Gaithersburg, MD 20877-4150
Tel: 301-990-7979
http://www.nbcot.org

# Occupational Therapy Assistants and Aides

## OVERVIEW

*Occupational therapy assistants* (also called *OTAs)* help people with mental, physical, developmental, or emotional limitations using a variety of activities to improve basic motor functions and reasoning abilities. They work under the direct supervision of an occupational therapist, and their duties include helping to plan, implement, and evaluate rehabilitation programs designed to regain patients' self-sufficiency and to restore their physical and mental functions. There are 26,600 occupational therapy assistants employed in the United States. *Occupational therapy aides* help OTAs and occupational therapists by doing such things as clerical work, preparing therapy equipment for a client's use, and keeping track of supplies. Approximately 7,800 occupational therapy aides are employed in the United States.

## HISTORY

Physicians have recognized the therapeutic value of providing activities and occupations for their patients since about the 14th century. Observations that mental patients tended to recover more quickly from their illnesses if provided with tasks and duties led physicians to involve their patients in such activities as agriculture, working with animals, weaving, and sewing. Over time, this practice became quite common, and the conditions of many patients were improved.

## QUICK FACTS

**School Subjects**
Health
Psychology

**Personal Skills**
Helping/teaching
Mechanical/manipulative

**Work Environment**
Primarily indoors
Primarily one location

**Minimum Education Level**
Associate's degree (assistants)
High school diploma (aides)

**Salary Range**
$33,350 to $50,250 to
$68,450+ (assistants)
$16,280 to $25,730 to
$47,590+ (aides)

**Certification or Licensing**
Required (assistants)
None available (aides)

**Outlook**
Much faster than the average

**DOT**
076

**GOE**
14.06.01

**NOC**
6631

**O*NET-SOC**
31-2011.00, 31-2012.00

Occupational therapy as we know it today had its beginning after World War I. The need to help disabled veterans of that war, and years later the veterans of World War II, stimulated the growth of this field. Even though its inception was in the psychiatric field, occupational therapy has developed an equally important role in other medical fields, including rehabilitation of physically disabled patients.

As more health care providers began to incorporate occupational therapy into their treatment philosophy, demand arose for workers who could assist occupational therapists with rehabilitation and office support services. Thus, the careers of occupational therapy assistant and occupational therapy aide were born. These health care professionals, who work under the direct supervision of occupational therapists, play an integral role in the care of people with mental, physical, developmental, or emotional limitations.

## THE JOB

Occupational therapy is used to help provide rehabilitation services to persons with mental, physical, emotional, or developmental disabilities. The goal of occupational therapy is to improve a patient's quality of life by compensating for limitations caused by age, illness, or injury. It differs from physical therapy because it focuses not only on physical rehabilitation, but also on psychological well-being. Occupational therapy emphasizes improvement of the activities of daily living—including such functions as personal hygiene, dressing, eating, and cooking.

Occupational therapy assistants, under the supervision of the therapist, implement patient care plans and activities. They help patients improve mobility and productivity using a variety of activities and exercises. They may use adaptive techniques and equipment to help patients perform tasks many take for granted. A reacher, a long-handled device that pinches and grabs small items, may be used to pick up keys from the floor or a book from the shelf. Therapy assistants may have patients mix ingredients for a cake or flip a grilled cheese sandwich using a special spatula. Activities such as dancing, playing cards, or throwing a ball are fun, yet they help improve mobility and give the patients a sense of self-esteem. Therapists evaluate an activity, minimize the number of steps, and streamline movement so the patient will be less fatigued.

Assistants may also help therapists evaluate a patient's progress, change care plans as needed, make therapy appointments, and complete paperwork.

Occupational therapy aides are responsible for materials and equipment used during therapy. They assemble and clean equipment and make certain the therapists and assistants have what they need for a patient's therapy session. A therapy aide's duties are more clerical in nature. They answer telephones, schedule appointments, order supplies and equipment, and complete insurance forms and other paperwork.

## REQUIREMENTS

### High School

According to the U.S. Department of Labor, most occupational therapy aides receive on-the-job training, while occupational therapy assistants require further education after high school. For either position, however, a high school diploma is a must. Prepare for these careers by taking classes in biology, health, and social sciences. Anyone interested in doing this work must also be able to communicate clearly, follow directions, and work as part of a team. English or communication classes can help you improve on these skills.

In addition, admissions officers at postsecondary programs are favorably impressed if you have experience in the health care field. If you cannot find a paid job, consider volunteering at a local hospital or nursing home during your high school years.

### Postsecondary Training

While occupational therapy aides receive on-the-job training, occupational therapy assistants must have an associate's degree from an accredited OTA program. Programs are accredited by the Accreditation Council for Occupational Therapy Education (ACOTE), which is part of the American Occupational Therapy Association (AOTA). Approximately 135 programs are fully accredited by the ACOTE; in addition, a number of programs are on "inactive status," meaning that they are not currently accepting new students but may reactivate (begin accepting students again) in the future. A full listing of programs, as well as their contact information, is available at http://www.aota.org/Students/Schools.aspx.

Generally, programs take two years to complete. Studies include courses such as human anatomy, psychology of adjustment, biology, gerontology, pediatrics, adult physical disabilities, human kinesiology, therapeutic media, and techniques. Most schools also require their students to take a number of general classes as well to round out their education. These may be courses such as English, business math, and management. In addition to classwork, you will be required to complete at least 16 weeks of supervised fieldwork, which will give you hands-on experience with occupational therapy.

## Certification or Licensing

Occupational therapy aides do not require certification or licensing. Occupational therapy assistants must pass the certifying test of the National Board for Certification in Occupational Therapy. After passing this test, assistants receive the designation certified occupational therapy assistant. Licensure requirements for assistants vary by state, so you will need to check with the licensing board of the state in which you want to work for specific information.

## Other Requirements

Occupational therapy assistants and aides must be able to take directions. OTAs should have a pleasant disposition, strong people skills, and a desire to help those in need. Assistants must also be patient and responsible. Aides, too, should be responsible. They also need to be detail oriented in order to keep track of paperwork and equipment. It is important for assistants and aides to work well as a team.

# EXPLORING

A visit to your local hospital's occupational therapy department is the best way to learn about this field. Speak with occupational therapists, assistants, and aides to gain an understanding of the work they do. Also, the AOTA and other related organizations might be able to provide career information. School guidance and job centers, and the library, are good information sources.

# EMPLOYERS

There are approximately 26,600 occupational therapy assistants and 7,800 occupational therapy aides employed in the United States. About 28 percent of all assistants and aides are employed in offices of other health care practitioners, 27 percent work in a hospital setting, 23 percent are employed by occupational therapists, and 20 percent work in nursing care facilities. Others work in community care facilities for the elderly, home health care services, outpatient rehabilitation centers, and government agencies.

# STARTING OUT

The career services department of your local community college or technical school can provide a listing of jobs available in the occupational therapy field. Job openings are usually posted in hospital human resource departments. Professional groups are also a good source of information; for example, the AOTA offers an employment site at http://aota.otjoblink.org.

## ADVANCEMENT

After some experience, occupational therapy assistants can be promoted to *lead assistant*. Lead assistants are responsible for making work schedules of other assistants and for training occupational therapy students. Since occupational therapy assistants work under the supervision of an occupational therapist, there is little room for advancement. Aides may return to school and train to become occupational therapy assistants. Some assistants and aides return to school to become occupational therapists. Some shift to other health care careers.

## EARNINGS

According to the U.S. Department of Labor, the median yearly income of occupational therapy assistants was $50,250 in 2009. Salaries ranged from less than $33,350 to $68,450 or more annually. Naturally, experience, location, and type of employer all factor into the salaries paid.

The importance of education, though, cannot be overlooked, as assistants tend to earn more than aides. Median annual earnings of occupational therapist aides were $25,730 in 2009, according to the U.S. Department of Labor. Salaries ranged from less than $16,280 to $47,590 or more annually.

Benefits for full-time workers depend on the employer. They generally include health and life insurance, paid sick and vacation time, holiday pay, and a retirement plan.

## WORK ENVIRONMENT

Most occupational therapy assistants and aides work during the day, although depending on the place of employment, some evening or weekend work may be required. Most therapy is done in a hospital or clinic setting that is clean, well lighted, and generally comfortable.

Occupational therapy assistants often use everyday items, settings, and activities to help rehabilitate their patients. Such props include kitchen settings, card games, dancing, or exercises. Therapy assistants should be in good physical shape, since heavy lifting—of patients as well as equipment—is a daily part of the job. Therapy assistants should also have stamina, since they are on their feet for much of the day.

# OUTLOOK

According to the *Occupational Outlook Handbook*, employment for occupational therapy assistants and aides will grow much faster than the average for all careers through 2018. However, only a small number of new jobs will actually be available due to the size of these occupations. Occupational growth will stem from an increased number of people with disabilities and elderly people. Although more people are living well into their 70s, 80s, and in some cases, 90s, they often need the kinds of services occupational therapy provides. Medical technology has greatly improved, saving many lives that in the past would be lost through accidents, stroke, or other illnesses. Such people need rehabilitation therapy as they recuperate. Hospitals and employers are hiring more therapy assistants to help with the workload and to reduce costs.

Occupational therapy aides with just a high school diploma will face increasingly strong competition for jobs as more aides pursue advanced education.

# FOR MORE INFORMATION

*For additional information on careers, education, and news related to the field, contact*
**American Occupational Therapy Association**
4720 Montgomery Lane
PO Box 31220
Bethesda, MD 20824-1220
Tel: 301-652-2682
http://www.aota.org

*For information on certification, contact*
**National Board for Certification in Occupational Therapy**
12 South Summit Avenue, Suite 100
Gaithersburg, MD 20877-4150
Tel: 301-990-7979
http://www.nbcot.org

# Orientation and Mobility Specialists

## OVERVIEW

*Orientation and mobility specialists* help people with disabilities stay actively involved in society. They teach blind, visually impaired, and disabled individuals how to master the skills necessary to live independently and often encourage them to participate in various educational or recreational programs. Specialists also serve as a source of information, referring clients to financial aid, benefits, and legal advice. These workers may be employed directly by an individual or indirectly through community planning, research, and publicity projects.

## HISTORY

Helping those with disabilities has long been a part of the social work profession. As early as 1657, facilities called almshouses provided shelter, food, and work to the poor and those with disabilities. In the mid-1800s, middle-class women referred to as "friendly visitors" visited the homes of poor families to instruct the disabled in household management, the pursuit of employment, and the education of children. However, these friendly visitors and other early charitable organizations were sometimes limited in whom they would serve, often providing help and information only to those with their same moral views and religious backgrounds.

People with severe disabilities were often confined to institutions. By the late 18th century, many states and counties had built these facilities, then referred to as insane asylums, for the 24-hour care of

### QUICK FACTS

**School Subjects**
Health
Psychology

**Personal Skills**
Communication/ideas
Helping/teaching

**Work Environment**
Primarily indoors
Primarily multiple locations

**Minimum Education Level**
Bachelor's degree

**Salary Range**
$28,600 to $46,300 to $71,190+

**Certification or Licensing**
Required by certain states

**Outlook**
Much faster than the average

**DOT**
076

**GOE**
14.06.01

**NOC**
4215

**O*NET-SOC**
29-1122.01

people suffering from afflictions ranging from mental retardation to paralysis. The patients of these hospitals were often committed against their will by relatives. Few efforts were made to help patients return to society to lead normal, active lives.

The settlement houses of the late 19th century, such as Jane Addams's Hull-House of Chicago, led to the development of more sensitive and enlightened ways to help people. Social workers lived among the residents, listening to and learning along with them. But even with this new understanding of social work, those with disabilities were still unable to get complete assistance. Society wanted to help those in need but didn't necessarily want to live among them. As a result, separate schools, workplaces, and agencies for the disabled were established. Although social workers instructed blind people in how to cook and clean, how to use a guide dog, and how to read Braille, they made few efforts to integrate them into the community.

Legal efforts to end this discrimination began in 1920 with the passing of the Vocational Rehabilitation Act. This act led to the development of state and federal agencies focused on enhancing the employment opportunities for people with disabilities. Over the years, this act has broadened to include job counseling and retraining services and the provision of prosthetic and other assisting devices. More recent efforts toward ending discrimination in employment and public services include the passing of the Americans with Disabilities Act of 1990.

## THE JOB

Although he was diagnosed with multiple sclerosis years ago, Ken Smith has only recently required the use of a wheelchair. He also has only partial use of his right hand. For the last few years, he has worked as a newspaper journalist, driving himself to crime scenes, taking notes during interviews, and writing at a frantic pace to keep up with the pace of the newsroom. Now that he requires a wheelchair to get around, he is going to have to make many adjustments in his life. Fortunately for Smith, there are a number of services and benefits to help him; he just needs to know how to find this help.

The simple act of providing information is one of the most important jobs of an orientation and mobility specialist. These workers help to direct people like Smith to the many agencies available that assist those with vision and mobility impairments. By listening carefully to the problem, orientation and mobility specialists determine the best route for assistance, contact the agency on behalf of the client, and make sure the client receives the proper assistance. Because of limited funding and support, disability services are often unable

# Books to Read

Falvo, Donna R. *Medical and Psychosocial Aspects of Chronic Illness and Disability.* 4th ed. Sudbury, Mass.: Jones & Bartlett Publishers, 2008.

Knott, Natalie Isaak. *Teaching Orientation and Mobility in the Schools: An Instructor's Companion.* New York: American Foundation for the Blind, 2002.

Mackelprang, Romel W., and Richard O. Salsgiver. *Disability: A Diversity Model Approach in Human Service Practice.* 2d ed. Chicago: Lyceum Books, 2009.

Motley, Ellavea Garrett. *The Role of the Teacher in Orientation and Mobility Services for the Visually Impaired.* Pittsburgh: Dorrance Publishing Company, 2002.

to promote themselves. The biggest problem facing communities is not the lack of services available, but the lack of public awareness of these outlets.

However, Smith will require much more than names and phone numbers from an orientation and mobility specialist. He not only needs to find the right wheelchair, but he also needs instruction on how to use it. His home needs to be analyzed to determine what modifications need to be made (for example, wheelchair ramps, handrails, and wider doorways). If the necessary modifications cannot be made, he will have to consider moving to a new place. For all of these somewhat daunting decisions, Smith can ask an orientation and mobility specialist for advice.

Smith's workplace may also require modifications. Though perfectly capable of continuing his work as a journalist, he is going to have to fulfill his duties in different ways. For example, a special car may be required. Because of the limited use of his hand, he may need a modified computer keyboard or an assistant. An orientation and mobility specialist can serve as a client's advocate, negotiating with employers to prevent any cause for discrimination in the workplace. Specialists may also offer training and education programs to integrate or reintegrate the client into the workplace.

An orientation and mobility specialist also serves as a counselor. A client may need individual therapy or a support group. The family of the client may also need counseling on how to adjust to a parent's or child's disability.

In addition to offering services that directly benefit the client (counseling, advocacy, education, and referral), some specialists may offer services that have indirect benefits for clients. These additional services include outreach, publicity, planning, and research. Because of a general lack of awareness of the social services available, orientation and mobility specialists may focus on ways to educate the public about the challenges facing those with disabilities. They may lead fund-raising efforts for research or programs aimed at assisting the disabled community.

# REQUIREMENTS

## High School

Because you will need a college degree and a well-rounded education, take your high school's program of college preparatory classes. These classes should include math and science courses as well as a foreign language. Strong communication skills are needed for this work, so to improve your skills in this area take four years of English. Speech and journalism classes are also beneficial. Courses in history, social studies, sociology, and psychology are also recommended.

Because a large part of the job is providing information about disability services, you should be comfortable using the Internet and various computer programs. Not only will you have to be able to work with computers yourself, you may be required to teach clients how to use them, too.

## Postsecondary Training

The Association for Education and Rehabilitation of the Blind and Visually Impaired (commonly known as AER) provides a listing of approved orientation and mobility programs at the graduate, undergraduate, and certification-only levels. Programs include instruction in mobility techniques, where students simulate blindness or limited vision with blindfolds or other devices. Internships with disability agencies are also incorporated into the programs.

Other specialists prepare themselves for the career by studying social work. The Council on Social Work Education requires that five areas be covered in accredited bachelor's degree social work programs: human behavior and the social environment, social welfare policy and services, social work practice, research, and field practicum. Most programs require two years of liberal arts study, followed by two years of study in the social work major. Also, students must complete a field practicum of at least 400 hours.

Though some starting positions require only a bachelor's degree, most supervisory and administrative positions within social work require further education. Graduate programs are organized according to fields of practice (e.g., mental health care), problem areas (e.g., substance abuse), population groups (e.g., the elderly), and practice roles (e.g., practice with individuals, families, or communities). They are usually two-year programs with at least 900 hours of field practice. Doctoral degrees are also available for those interested in research, planning, or community outreach jobs.

### Certification or Licensing
Only selected states require orientation and mobility specialists to be certified. The Academy for Certification of Vision Rehabilitation and Education Professionals offers certification for orientation and mobility specialists who meet certain educational and experience requirements. To be eligible to sit for the certification exam, individuals must first complete an AER-approved orientation and mobility program. Applicants who meet these certification requirements can use the designation of certified orientation and mobility specialist. Certification is also available in low vision therapy and vision rehabilitation therapy.

### Other Requirements
For years, people with disabilities have faced discrimination. This discrimination is fueled by fear, by misunderstanding, and by the way people with disabilities are represented in popular culture. Orientation and mobility specialists must be able to honestly address their own perceptions of people with disabilities. Specialists must be sensitive to the client's situation and have a genuine interest in involving that person in the community and workplace.

Specialists also work frequently with the elderly, which requires understanding the aging experience. Workers must be patient and be good listeners to provide the elderly with the supportive network they need.

Communication skills are also very important. Much of the work as an orientation and mobility specialist involves talking and listening to clients, teaching, interviewing, and counseling. You will need to provide clear instructions to clients, their families, and their employers.

Because many of the problems facing those with disabilities stem from discrimination, many specialists work to educate the public about living with disabilities through research, reports, and fundraising. Being comfortable talking to a variety of people and in a variety of settings is an asset for these specialists.

## EXPLORING
To learn more about this work, you can explore Web sites concerning disabilities and social work. A job in the school or public library

helping people conduct research will put your information retrieval skills to good use. Working on the school newspaper will also help you develop your writing, researching, and interviewing skills, all important aspects of social work.

Part-time data entry jobs at a hospital or long-term care facility can familiarize you with medical terminology and the services available to people with disabilities. A part-time job in a retail pharmacy will involve you directly with people with disabilities and also the services that pay for the rental and purchase of wheelchairs, walkers, and canes. You can also gain experience by volunteering at any social service agency to get a sense of the work environment and responsibilities.

## EMPLOYERS

Orientation and mobility specialists can find work with for-profit, nonprofit, and public programs. They may work in hospitals and community agencies such as transitional living services or with private agencies that focus on providing services specifically to those with disabilities.

An orientation and mobility specialist may also be self-employed, providing service on a contract basis to individuals or social service agencies.

## STARTING OUT

To gain experience in social work, consider working with a social service agency specializing in information and referral. Rehabilitation centers, senior homes, schools, and summer camps for the blind, visually impaired, and disabled also offer many opportunities for experience. Because of limited funding, staffing may consist of only a few social work professionals, and the rest may be volunteers or assistants. Volunteer work may lead to full-time employment or simply introduce you to other social work professionals who can provide career guidance and letters of reference.

## ADVANCEMENT

Orientation and mobility specialists may advance to become supervisors of assistants or executive directors of rehabilitation agencies. Another possible route for advancement is through teaching.

The more challenging and better-paying jobs tend to go to those with more years of practical experience and higher degrees. Further study, extensive experience, and good references will lead to advancement in the profession. Also, many social work programs offer continuing education workshops, courses, and seminars. These refresher courses help practicing specialists refine their skills and learn about new areas of practice, methods, and problems. These courses are intended to supplement previous education, not substitute for a bachelor's or master's degree. Continuing education can lead to job promotions and salary increases.

## EARNINGS

The higher the degree held by specialists, the higher their earning potential. Those with a Ph.D. can take jobs in indirect service, research, and planning. Salaries also vary among regions; in general, social workers on the East and West Coasts earn higher salaries than those in the Midwest. During the first five years of practice, salaries increase faster than in later years.

Medical and public health social workers (a category that includes orientation and mobility specialists) earned a median annual salary of $46,300 in 2009, according to the U.S. Department of Labor. The lowest paid 10 percent earned less than $28,600 and the highest paid 10 percent earned more than $71,190.

Specialists who work in school systems are generally paid on the same scale as teachers in the system. Those who work for private clients are usually paid by the hour or per session.

Orientation and mobility specialists usually receive benefits such as vacation days, sick leave, health and life insurance, and a savings and pension program. Self-employed specialists must provide their own benefits.

## WORK ENVIRONMENT

Orientation and mobility specialists work part of the time in an office, analyzing and updating client files, interviewing clients over the phone, and talking with other service agencies. Depending on the size of the agency, office duties such as typing letters, filing, and answering phones may be performed by an aide or volunteer.

The rest of their time is spent outside the office, interacting directly with clients and others. Orientation and mobility specialists are involved directly with the people they serve and must carefully examine their clients' living conditions and family relations.

Advocacy involves work in a variety of different environments; it involves meetings with clients' employers, agency directors, and local legislators. Should the client press charges for discrimination, orientation and mobility specialists may be called upon to testify in court.

Both counseling and advocacy can be stressful aspects of the work, but helping to empower people with disabilities can be very rewarding.

## OUTLOOK

According to the U.S. Census Bureau, more than 54 million people (approximately 19 percent of Americans) had a disability in 2008. In addition to continuing the fight against discrimination in the workplace and in general society, the disabled also need assistance in order to live productive lives.

Future funding is an important consideration for social service agencies. In many cases, the agencies providing information and referral must compete for funding with the very programs to which they refer people. This calls for good relationships between agencies and services. In order for agencies to receive adequate funding, social workers, including orientation and mobility specialists, must conduct research and provide reports to federal, state, and local governments showing proof of financial need. Their reports help to illustrate where funds should be allocated to best serve the disabled community.

According to the U.S. Department of Labor, the employment of social workers, including those who work with the visually and physically impaired, is expected to increase much faster than the average for all occupations through 2018. Specialists will continue to increase public awareness of the importance of aid for the disabled and visually impaired. Assistance services will continue to make their way into more areas, such as workplaces, libraries, and other public facilities.

New computer technology will continue to cater to the special needs of the disabled. The development of specialized equipment and the expansion of Internet resources allow the disabled and visually impaired to access online resources for assistance. Orientation and mobility specialists will be needed to help those with disabilities use new technology to their best advantage.

## FOR MORE INFORMATION

For information on certification, contact
    **Academy for Certification of Vision Rehabilitation and Education Professionals**
    3333 North Campbell Avenue, Suite 2
    Tucson, AZ 85719-2361
    Tel: 520-887-6816
    http://www.acvrep.org

*For resources and advocacy for the disabled community, contact*
American Association of People with Disabilities
1629 K Street, NW, Suite 950
Washington, DC 20006-1675
Tel: 800-840-8844
http://www.aapd.com

*For information on educational programs, contact*
Association for Education and Rehabilitation of the Blind and
   Visually Impaired
1703 North Beauregard Street, Suite 440
Alexandria, VA 22311-1744
Tel: 877-492-2708
http://www.aerbvi.org

*To read frequently asked questions about how to become a social
worker, check out the following Web site:*
Council on Social Work Education
1701 Duke Street, Suite 200
Alexandria, VA 22314-3415
Tel: 703-683-8080
E-mail: info@cswe.org
http://www.cswe.org

*For information about careers, education, and job leads, contact*
National Association of Social Workers
750 First Street, NE, Suite 700
Washington, DC 20002-4241
Tel: 202-408-8600
http://www.socialworkers.org

# Psychiatric Technicians

## QUICK FACTS

**School Subjects**
Health
Psychology

**Personal Skills**
Communication/ideas
Helping/teaching

**Work Environment**
Primarily indoors
Primarily one location

**Minimum Education Level**
Some postsecondary training

**Salary Range**
$18,140 to $28,140 to
$50,140+

**Certification or Licensing**
Required by certain states
and employers

**Outlook**
More slowly than average

**DOT**
079

**GOE**
14.07.01

**NOC**
3413

**O*NET-SOC**
29-2053.00, 31-1013.00

## OVERVIEW

*Psychiatric technicians*, also known as *psychiatric aides, mental health assistants*, and *psychiatric nursing assistants*, work with mentally ill, emotionally disturbed, or developmentally disabled people. Their duties vary considerably depending on place of work but may include helping patients with hygiene and housekeeping and recording patients' pulses, temperatures, and respiration rates. Psychiatric technicians participate in treatment programs by having one-on-one sessions with patients, sometimes under a nurse's or counselor's direction.

Another prime aspect of the psychiatric technician's work is reporting observations of patients' behavior to medical and psychiatric staff. Psychiatric technicians may also fill out admitting forms for new patients, contact patients' families to arrange conferences, issue medications from the dispensary, and maintain records. There are approximately 57,100 psychiatric technicians employed in the United States.

## HISTORY

Although some mentally ill people were treated as early as the 15th century in institutions like the Hospital of Saint Mary of Bethlehem in London (whose name was often shortened to Bedlam), the practice of institutionalizing people with mental disorders did not become common until the 17th century.

During the 17th, 18th, and even into the 19th centuries, treatment of mentally ill patients was quite crude and often simply barbarous. This state of affairs started to change as medical practitioners began

# Words to Know

**Neurosis:** A mental and emotional disorder that affects only part of the personality. A neurosis does not disturb the use of language, and it is accompanied by various physical, physiological, and mental disturbances, the most usual being anxieties or phobias.

**Obsessive-compulsive:** A neurosis that results in the patient's compulsion to carry out certain acts, no matter how odd or illogical or repetitive they are. This sort of neurosis is evident once the obsession or compulsive act interferes with normal life. For example, a person obsessed with cleanliness might take a dozen or more showers a day.

**Paranoid schizophrenic:** The most common and destructive of the psychotic disorders, characterized by departure from reality, inability to think clearly, difficulty feeling and expressing emotions, and a retreat into a fantasy life.

**Phobias:** Irrational or overblown fears that prevent a person from living a normal life.

**Psychosis:** A more complete disintegration of personality and loss of contact with the outside world than with neurosis.

to see mental illness as a medical problem. During the late 18th and early 19th centuries, hospitals began concentrating on keeping patients clean and comfortable, building their self-respect, and treating them with friendliness and encouragement. This method of treating mental illness resulted in the establishment of specially designed institutions for the care of mental patients.

Beginning in the 1940s, mental health institutions sought more effective therapeutic services for their patients, including more social activities and innovative treatment programs. Treatment shifted from a sole reliance on state mental hospitals to provision of more services in general hospitals and community mental health centers.

The object was to shorten periods of institutionalization and to decrease the stigma and dislocation associated with treatment in mental hospitals. However, these changes also sharply increased personnel needs. One strategy for dealing with this has been to train more professionals: psychiatrists, psychologists, social workers, nurses, and others. Another strategy has focused on training more nonprofessionals: aides, attendants, orderlies, and others.

The drive to develop new therapies and the trend toward deinstitutionalizing patients have led to the creation of a new category of mental health worker with a training level between that of the professional and the nonprofessional. Workers at this level are usually referred to as paraprofessionals or technicians, and in the mental health field they are known as psychiatric technicians or *mental health technicians.*

## THE JOB

Psychiatric technicians not only take over for or work with professionals in traditional treatment activities but also provide new services in innovative ways.

They may work with alcohol and drug abusers, psychotic or emotionally disturbed children and adults, developmentally disabled people, or the aged. They must be skilled and specially trained.

Psychiatric technicians are supervised by registered nurses, counselors, therapists, or, more and more frequently, senior psychiatric technicians. Psychiatric technicians work as part of a team of mental health care workers and provide physical and mental rehabilitation for patients through recreational, occupational, and psychological readjustment programs.

In general, psychiatric technicians help plan and implement individual treatment programs. Specific activities vary according to work setting, but they may include the following: interviewing and information gathering; working in a hospital unit admitting, screening, evaluating, or discharging patients; record keeping; making referrals to community agencies; working for patients' needs and rights; visiting patients at home after their release from a hospital; and participating in individual and group counseling and therapy.

Psychiatric technicians endeavor to work with patients in a broad, comprehensive manner and to see each patient as a person whose peculiar or abnormal behavior stems from an illness or disability. They strive to help each patient achieve a maximum level of functioning. This means helping patients strengthen social and mental skills, accept greater responsibility, and develop confidence to enter into social, educational, or vocational activities.

In addition, psychiatric technicians working in hospitals handle a certain number of nursing responsibilities. They may take temperature, pulse and respiration rates; measure blood pressure; and help administer medications and physical treatments. In many cases, technicians working in hospitals will find themselves concerned with all aspects of their patients' lives—from eating, sleeping, and personal hygiene to developing social skills and improving self-image.

Technicians working in clinics, community mental health centers, halfway houses, day hospitals, or other noninstitutional settings also perform some activities special to their situation. They interview newly registered patients and patients' relatives and visit patients and their families at home. They also administer psychological tests, participate in group activities, and write reports about their observations to supervising psychiatrists or other mental health professionals. They try to ease the transition of patients leaving hospitals and returning to their communities. They may refer patients to and arrange for consultations with mental health specialists. They may also help patients resolve problems with employment, housing, and personal finance.

Most psychiatric technicians are trained as generalists in providing mental health services. But some opportunities exist for technicians to specialize in a particular aspect of mental health care. For example, some psychiatric technicians specialize in the problems of mentally disturbed children. Others work as counselors in drug and alcohol abuse programs or as members of psychiatric emergency or crisis-intervention teams.

Another area of emphasis is working in community mental health. Technicians employed in this area are sometimes known as *human services technicians*. They use rehabilitation techniques for non-hospitalized patients who have problems adjusting to their social environment. These technicians may be primarily concerned with drug and alcohol abuse, parental effectiveness, the elderly, or problems in interpersonal relationships. Human services technicians work in social welfare departments, child care centers, preschools, vocational rehabilitation workshops, and schools for the learning disabled, emotionally disturbed, and mentally disabled. This concentration is particularly popular in college curricula, according to the American Association of Psychiatric Technicians (AAPT), although it has yet to find wide acceptance in the job market.

With slightly different training, psychiatric technicians may specialize in the treatment of developmentally disabled people. These technicians, sometimes referred to as *DD techs*, work with patients by doing such things as teaching recreational activities. They generally work in halfway houses, state hospitals, training centers, or state and local service agencies.

Ellen Lantosh works as a psychiatric technician for the California Department of Developmental Services at Sonoma Developmental Center in Sonoma County, California. "My entire career has involved working with the behaviorally challenged," she says. "I started in 1976. I've been at Sonoma Developmental Center for 17 years. My previous experience was at Camarillo State Hospital in

Adolescence Admission. Psychiatric technicians are highly trained professionals who do the work many see as beneath them, or who many wonder, 'Who does do that work?' There are people in powerful positions who ought to come visit and work like we do for a few days. It might be a surprise how hard we work, yet keep the laughter alive and keep fun in our hearts. I've improved a few lives. I've also saved a few lives. It's all just part of the day."

## REQUIREMENTS

### High School

A high school diploma is the minimum education requirement to find work as a psychiatric technician, although in many cases psychiatric technicians are expected to have two years of training beyond high school. In general, high school students should take courses in English, biology, psychology, and sociology.

### Postsecondary Training

The two-year postsecondary training programs usually lead to an associate of arts or associate of science degree. It is important to note that many hospitals prefer to hire applicants with bachelor's degrees.

In general, study programs include human development, personality structure, the nature of mental illness, and, to a limited extent, anatomy, physiology, basic nursing, and medical science. Other subjects usually include some introduction to basic social sciences so that technicians can better understand relevant family and community structures, an overview of the structure and functions of institutions that treat patients, and most importantly, practical instruction.

Most mental health technology programs emphasize interviewing skills. Interview training enables technicians to observe and record accurately a patient's tone of voice and body language; this data will then be interpreted by the treatment team and sometimes even a court of law. Some programs also teach administration of selected psychological tests. You may also gain knowledge and training in crisis intervention techniques, child guidance, group counseling, family therapy, behavior modification, and consultation skills.

### Certification or Licensing

Voluntary certification is available through the American Association of Psychiatric Technicians. To receive certification, you will need to take an exam covering topics on mental disorders and developmental disabilities. Those who pass the test receive the designation nationally certified psychiatric technician and can place the initials

NCPT after their names. Depending on the employer, a certified technician may qualify for higher pay than a noncertified worker.

Psychiatric technicians must be licensed in California, Colorado, Kansas, and Arkansas. Ask your guidance or career services counselors for more information about licensing requirements in your state.

## Other Requirements

Because psychiatric technicians interact with people, you must be sensitive to others' needs and feelings. Some aspects of sensitivity can be learned, but this requires a willingness to listen, being extremely observant, and risking involvement in situations that at first may seem ambiguous and confusing. In addition, you need to be willing to look at your own attitudes and behaviors and to be flexible and open about effecting changes in them. The more you know about yourself, the more effective you will be in helping others.

Patience, understanding, and a "thick skin" are required in working with people who may be disagreeable and unpleasant because of their illnesses. Patients can be particularly adept at finding a person's weaknesses and exploiting them. This is not a job for the tenderhearted. A sense of responsibility and the ability to remain calm in emergencies are also essential characteristics.

# EXPLORING

Prospective psychiatric technicians can gather personal experience in this field in a number of ways. You can apply for a job as a nurse's aide at a local general hospital. In this way you gain direct experience providing patient care. If such a job requires too much of a time commitment, you might consider volunteering at a hospital part time or during the summer. Volunteering is an excellent way to become acquainted with the field, and many techs' full-time jobs evolve from volunteer positions. Most volunteers must be 21 years of age to work in the mental health unit. Younger students who are interested in volunteering can often find places in the medical records department or other areas to get their feet in the door.

People interested in this career might also consider volunteering at their local mental health association or a local social welfare agency. In some cases, the mental health association can arrange opportunities for volunteer work inside a mental hospital or mental health clinic. Finally, either on your own or with your teachers, you can arrange a visit to a mental health clinic. You may be able to talk with staff members and observe firsthand how psychiatric technicians do their jobs.

## EMPLOYERS

Approximately 57,100 psychiatric technicians are employed in the United States. About 50 percent work in hospitals. Others are employed at community mental health centers, psychiatric clinics, schools and day centers for the developmentally disabled, and social service agencies. They also work at residential and nonresidential centers, such as geriatric nursing homes, child or adolescent development centers, and halfway houses. Other potential places of employment for psychiatric technicians include correctional programs and juvenile courts, schools for the blind and deaf, community action programs, family service centers, and public housing programs.

## STARTING OUT

Graduates from mental health and human services technology programs can usually choose from a variety of job possibilities. College career services offices can be extremely helpful in locating employment. Students can follow want ads or apply directly to the clinics, agencies, or hospitals of their choice. Job information can also be obtained from the department of mental health in each state.

Ellen Lantosh's first job was on the Penal Code Receiving Unit at Patton State Hospital in San Bernardino County, California. "I did the admission and discharge summaries and plans, and also did exercise and relaxation techniques," she recalls. "Young people miss out on the entry level of this employment. It's a great start for those who are looking for direction. There are a number of opportunities if you look around. No one is stuck in any one place if they don't want to be; transfer opportunities are available statewide."

## ADVANCEMENT

Working as a psychiatric technician is still a relatively new occupation, and sequences of promotions have not yet been clearly defined in some settings. Seeking national certification through the AAPT is one way to help set up a career path in this field. Advancement normally takes the form of being given greater responsibilities with less supervision. It usually results from gaining experience, developing competence and leadership abilities, and continuing formal and practical education. In cases where promotions are governed by civil service regulations, advancement is based on experience and test scores on promotion examinations.

In large part, advancement is linked to gaining further education. Thus, after working a few years, technicians may decide to obtain a bachelor's degree in psychology. Advanced education, coupled with previous training and work experience, greatly enhance advancement potential. For instance, with a bachelor's degree, experienced technicians may be able to find rewarding positions as instructors in programs to train future mental health workers.

## EARNINGS

Salaries for psychiatric technicians vary according to geographical area and work setting: technicians in California generally receive substantially higher wages than those in other areas of the country, and technicians in community settings generally receive higher salaries than those in institutional settings. The U.S. Department of Labor reports that psychiatric technicians earned median annual salaries of $28,140 in 2009. The lowest paid 10 percent earned less than $18,140, and the highest paid 10 percent earned $50,140 or more.

Most psychiatric technicians receive fringe benefits, including health insurance, sick leave, and paid vacations. Technicians working for state institutions or agencies will probably also be eligible for financial assistance for further education.

## WORK ENVIRONMENT

Psychiatric technicians work in a variety of settings, and their working conditions vary accordingly. Typically they work 40 hours a week, five days a week, although one may be a weekend day. Some psychiatric technicians work evening or night shifts, and all technicians may sometimes be asked to work holidays.

For the most part, the physical surroundings are pleasant. Most institutions, clinics, mental health centers, and agency offices are kept clean and comfortably furnished. Technicians who work with the mentally ill must nonetheless adjust to an environment that is normally chaotic and sometimes upsetting. Some patients are acutely depressed and withdrawn or excessively agitated and excited. Some patients may become unexpectedly violent and verbally abusive. However, institutions treating these kinds of patients maintain enough staff to keep the patients safe and to protect workers from physical harm. Psychiatric technicians who make home visits also may sometimes confront unpleasant conditions.

Finally, psychiatric technicians work not only with individuals but also often with the community. In that role, technicians can be called upon to advocate for their patients by motivating community agencies to provide services or by obtaining exceptions to rules when needed for individuals or groups of patients. Successful psychiatric technicians become competent in working and dealing with various decision-making processes of community and neighborhood groups.

## OUTLOOK

The U.S. Department of Labor projects that employment for psychiatric technicians will grow more slowly than the average for all careers through 2018. Despite this prediction, demand for technicians is expected to continue, and even grow, in large part because of a well-established trend of returning hospitalized patients to their communities after shorter and shorter periods of hospitalization. This trend has encouraged development of comprehensive community mental health centers and has led to a strong demand for psychiatric technicians to staff these facilities. Tony Myers, president of the California Association of Psychiatric Technicians and a senior psychiatric technician at Lanterman Developmental Center in Pomona, California, sees positive employment prospects for psychiatric technicians. "With growing populations of people with mental illnesses and developmental disabilities, plus increasing rehabilitation programs in correctional facilities, we actually predict a rising demand for psychiatric technicians throughout the nation."

Concerns over rising health care costs should increase employment levels for technicians, because they and other paraprofessionals can take over some functions of higher paid professionals. This kind of substitution has been proven to be an effective way of reducing costs without reducing quality of care.

## FOR MORE INFORMATION

*For information on becoming a nationally certified psychiatric technician, contact*
**American Association of Psychiatric Technicians**
1220 S Street, Suite 100
Sacramento, CA 95811-7138
Tel: 800-391-7589
http://www.psychtechs.org

*For more information on the career, contact*
**California Association of Psychiatric Technicians**
1220 S Street, Suite 100
Sacramento, CA 95811-7138
Tel: 800-677-2278
http://www.psychtechs.net

# Psychiatrists

## OVERVIEW

Psychiatrists are physicians who attend to patients' mental, emotional, and behavioral symptoms. They try to help people function better in their daily lives. Different kinds of psychiatrists use different treatment methods depending on their fields. They may explore a patient's beliefs and history. They may prescribe medicine, including tranquilizers, antipsychotics, and antidepressants. If they specialize in treating children, they may use play therapy.

## HISTORY

The greatest advances in psychiatric treatment came in the latter part of the 19th century. Emil Kraepelin, a German psychiatrist, made an important contribution when he developed a classification system for mental illnesses that is still used for diagnosis. Sigmund Freud, the famous Viennese psychiatrist, developed techniques for analyzing human behavior that have strongly influenced the practice of modern psychiatry. Freud first lectured in the United States in 1909. Swiss psychiatrist Carl Jung, a former associate of Freud's, revolutionized the field with his theory of a collective unconscious.

Another great change in treatment began in the 1950s with the development of medication that could be used in treating psychiatric problems, such as depression and anxiety.

# Words to Know

**Affect:** A person's emotional state or mood, which one feels and which can be observed by others; mood disorders are also called affective disorders.

**Compulsion:** An often-irresistible urge to perform or repeat a certain action, driven by a person's obsession with an idea or situation.

**Idealization:** An inaccurate perception that ascribes disproportionately positive aspects to a person or place or idea.

**Psychoanalysis:** A method of treating mental disorders by bringing unconscious fears and conflicts into the conscious mind.

**Psychosomatic:** A physical illness caused or aggravated by a mental condition.

**Psychotherapy:** The treatment of mental disorders by psychological, rather than physical, means.

## THE JOB

Psychiatrists are medical doctors (M.D.s) who treat people suffering from mental and emotional illnesses. Problems treated range from being irritable and feeling frustrated to losing touch with reality. Some people, in addition to having a mental illness, may also engage in destructive behavior, such as abusing alcohol or drugs or committing crimes. Others may have physical symptoms that spring from mental or emotional disorders. People with mental illness were once so misunderstood and stigmatized by society that they were kept, chained and shackled, in asylums. Today, society recognizes that emotional or mental illnesses need to be diagnosed and treated just like any other medical problem.

Some psychiatrists run general practices, treating patients with a variety of mental disorders. Others may specialize in working with certain types of therapy or kinds of patients, for example, the chronically ill. When meeting a client for the first time, psychiatrists conduct an evaluation of the client. This involves talking with the person about his or her current circumstances and getting a medical history. In some cases, the psychiatrist will give the client a physical examination or order laboratory tests if he or she feels the client's problem may have a physical cause. Next, the psychiatrist decides on a treatment plan for the client. This may involve medications, psychotherapy, or a combination of these.

As medical doctors, psychiatrists can prescribe medication that affects a client's mood or behavior, such as tranquilizers or antidepressants. Scientific advancements in both the understanding of how the human brain functions and the creation of more effective drugs with fewer side effects have helped make medications an important element in the treatment of mental illness. Some psychiatrists will only supervise the medication aspect of a client's treatment and refer the client to another health professional, such as a *psychologist,* for the psychotherapy aspect of treatment. These psychiatrists often work in private practices and focus on the chemical aspects of a person's illness to find medication to help that client. Other psychiatrists, often those working in hospitals or in small cities and towns, may be the providers of both medication management and psychotherapy.

Psychotherapy, sometimes called *talk therapy,* is perhaps the most well-known type of treatment for mental illness, conjuring images of the patient on the couch while the psychiatrist takes copious notes. Although these elements of talk therapy are sometimes exaggerated in film and on television, the depiction of talk therapy as talking is basically correct. By having the client talk about problems he or she faces, the therapist helps the client uncover and understand the feelings and ideas that form the root of the client's problems and, thus, overcome emotional pain. Talk therapy can be used with individuals, groups, couples, or families.

Another therapy method used by some psychiatrists is *behavior therapy* or *behavior modification therapy.* This therapy focuses on changing a client's behavior and may involve teaching the client to use meditation and relaxation techniques as well as other treatment methods, such as biofeedback, a process in which a person uses electronic monitors to measure the effects that thoughts and feelings have on bodily functions like muscle tension, heart rate, or brain waves. This is done so that the client can learn how to consciously control his or her body through stress reduction.

*Free association* is a technique in which the client is encouraged to relax and talk freely. The therapist's aim is to help the client uncover troubling subconscious beliefs or conflicts and their causes. Dreams may also be examined for hints about the unconscious mind. Subconscious conflicts are believed to cause neurosis, which is an emotional disorder in which the patient commonly exhibits anxious behavior.

Besides seeing clients, psychiatrists may also work with other health care professionals in the course of treatment.

In addition to those working in general psychiatry, there are psychiatrists who specialize in working with certain groups or in certain areas. These specialists include the following.

*Child psychiatrists* work with youth and usually their parents as well.

At the opposite end of the age scale are *geriatric psychiatrists,* who specialize in working with older individuals.

*Industrial psychiatrists* are employed by companies to deal with problems that affect employee performance, such as alcoholism or absenteeism.

*Forensic psychiatrists* work in the field of law. They evaluate defendants and testify on their mental state. They may help determine whether or not defendants understand the charges against them and if they can contribute to their own defense.

Other health professionals who may work with mentally ill people include *psychologists*, who may see clients but are unable to prescribe medications because they are not physicians, and *neurologists*, physicians specializing in problems of the nervous system. In some cases, a person's disturbed behavior results from disorders of the nervous system, and neurologists diagnose and treat these conditions.

## REQUIREMENTS

### High School

Start preparing yourself for college and medical school while you are still in high school. Do this by taking a college preparatory curriculum and concentrating on math and science classes. Biology, chemistry, and physics as well as algebra, geometry, and calculus will all be helpful. You can also start learning about human behavior by taking psychology, sociology, and history classes. In addition, take English classes to develop your communication skills—much of this work involves speaking, listening, and record keeping.

### Postsecondary Training

When you are deciding what college to attend, keep in mind that you'll want one with a strong science department, excellent laboratory facilities, and a strong humanities department. You may want to check out the publication *Medical School Admissions Requirements* (http://www.aamc.org/students/applying/msar.htm) by the Association of American Medical Colleges (AAMC) to see what specific college classes you should take in preparation for medical school. Some colleges or universities offer a premed major; other possible majors include chemistry and biology. No matter what your major, though, you can count on taking biology, chemistry, organic chemistry, physics, and psychology classes. Medical schools look for well-rounded individuals, however, so be sure to take other classes in the humanities and social sciences. The

AAMC reports that most people apply to medical school after their junior year of college. Most medical schools require the Medical College Admission Test (http://www.aamc.org/students/mcat/start. htm) as part of their application, so you should take this test in your junior or even sophomore year.

In medical school, students must complete a four-year program of medical studies and supervised clinical work leading to their M.D. degrees. Students will once again concentrate on studying the sciences during their first two years; in addition, they will learn about taking a person's medical history and how to do an examination. The next two years are devoted to clinical work, which is when students first begin to see patients under supervision.

After receiving an M.D., physicians who plan to specialize in psychiatry must complete a residency. In the first year, they work in several specialties, such as internal medicine and pediatrics. Then they work for three years in a psychiatric hospital or a general hospital's psychiatric ward. Here they learn how to diagnose and treat various mental and emotional disorders or illnesses. Some psychiatrists continue their education beyond this four-year residency. To become a child psychiatrist, for example, a doctor must train for at least three years in general residency and two years in child psychiatry residency. Part of psychiatrists' training involves undergoing therapy themselves.

Psychiatrists can also attend an osteopathic medical program leading to the Doctor of Osteopathic Medicine degree.

### Certification or Licensing

Upon completion of residency training, psychiatrists may seek certification from the American Board of Psychiatry and Neurology (ABPN). To be eligible for certification, qualified applicants must have an unrestricted state license to practice medicine; have the required years of residency training; and must pass both a written and oral examination as administered by the ABPN.

All physicians must be licensed in order to practice medicine. After completing the M.D., graduates must pass the licensing test given by the board of medical examiners for the state in which they want to work.

### Other Requirements

To complete the required studies and training, students need outstanding mental ability and perseverance. Psychiatrists must be emotionally stable so they can deal with their patients objectively. Psychiatrists must be perceptive, able to listen well, and able to work well with others. They must also be dedicated to a lifetime of learning, as new therapeutic techniques and medications are constantly being developed.

## EXPLORING

You can easily explore this job by reading as much as you can about the field and the work. To find out what professionals consider worthwhile resources, you may want to read the *Authoritative Guide to Self-Help Resources in Mental Health* by John Norcross and others (New York: The Guilford Press, 2003). To learn about different types of psychotherapies, you may want to read *Essential Psychotherapies: Theory and Practice*, 2d ed., edited by Alan Gurman and Stanley Messer (New York: The Guilford Press, 2005). Talk with your counselor or psychology teacher about helping you arrange an information interview with a local psychiatrist. If this is not possible, try to get an information interview with any physician, such as your family doctor, to ask about the medical school experience.

An excellent way to explore this type of work is to do volunteer work in health care settings, such as hospitals, clinics, or nursing homes. While you may not be taking care of people with psychiatric problems, you will be interacting with patients and health care professionals. This experience will benefit you when it's time to apply to medical schools as well as give you a feel for working with the ill.

As a college student, you may be able to find a summer job as a hospital orderly, nurse's aide, or ward clerk.

## EMPLOYERS

Approximately half of practicing psychiatrists work in private practice; many others combine private practice with work in a health care institution. These institutions include private hospitals, state mental hospitals, medical schools, community health centers, and government health agencies. Psychiatrists may also work at correctional facilities, for health maintenance organizations, or in nursing homes. They are employed throughout the country.

## STARTING OUT

Psychiatrists in residency can find job leads in professional journals and through professional organizations such as the American Psychiatric Association. Many are offered permanent positions with the same institution where they complete their residency.

## ADVANCEMENT

Most psychiatrists advance in their careers by enlarging their knowledge and skills, clientele, and earnings. Those who work in hospitals, clinics, and mental health centers may become administrators. Those who teach or concentrate on research may become department heads.

## EARNINGS

Psychiatrists' earnings are determined by the kind of practice they have and its location, their experience, and the number of patients they treat. Like other physicians, their average income is among the highest of any occupation.

First-year medical interns earned $47,458 in 2009, according to the Association of American Medical Colleges. Psychiatrists earned median annual salaries of $160,230 in 2009, according to the U.S. Department of Labor. Salaries for psychiatrists ranged from $110,000 for those in their first year of practice to $189,499 for those in practice three years or longer, according to a salary survey by PhysiciansSearch.com.

Psychiatrists who are employed by health care institutions receive fringe benefits such as health insurance and paid vacation and sick days. Those who are self-employed must provide their own benefits.

## WORK ENVIRONMENT

Psychiatrists in private practice set their own schedules and usually work regular hours. They may work some evenings or weekends to see patients who cannot take time off during business hours. Most psychiatrists, however, put in long workdays, averaging 52 hours a week, according to the American Medical Association. Like other physicians, psychiatrists are always on call.

Psychiatrists in private practice typically work in comfortable office settings. Some private psychiatrists also work as hospital staff members, consultants, lecturers, or teachers.

Salaried psychiatrists work in private hospitals, state hospitals, and community mental health centers. They also work for government agencies, such as the U.S. Department of Health and Human Services, the Department of Defense, and the Department of Veterans Affairs. Psychiatrists who work in public facilities often bear heavy workloads. Changes in treatment have reduced the number of patients in hospitals and have increased the number of patients in community health centers.

# OUTLOOK

The U.S. Department of Labor predicts that employment for physicians will grow much faster than the average for all careers through 2018. Opportunities for psychiatrists in private practice and salaried positions are good. Demand is great for child psychiatrists, and other specialties are also in short supply, especially in rural areas and public facilities.

A number of factors contribute to this shortage. Growing population and increasing life span add up to more people who need psychiatric care; rising incomes enable more people to afford treatment; and higher educational levels make more people aware of the importance of mental health care. Medical insurance, although it usually limits the amount of mental health care, may provide some coverage.

Psychiatrists are also needed as researchers to explore the causes of mental illness and develop new ways to treat it.

# FOR MORE INFORMATION

*For information on forensic psychiatry, contact*
**American Academy of Psychiatry and the Law**
One Regency Drive
PO Box 30
Bloomfield, CT 06002-0030
Tel: 860-242-5450
http://www.aapl.org

*For information on geriatric psychiatry, contact*
**American Association for Geriatric Psychiatry**
7910 Woodmont Avenue, Suite 1050
Bethesda, MD 20814-3004
Tel: 301-654-7850
E-mail: main@aagponline.org
http://www.aagpgpa.org

*For information on board certification, contact*
**American Board of Psychiatry and Neurology**
2150 East Lake Cook Road, Suite 900
Buffalo Grove, IL 60089-1875
Tel: 847-229-6500
http://www.abpn.com

*For more information on becoming a doctor as well as current health care news, visit the association's Web site.*
**American Medical Association**
515 North State Street
Chicago, IL 60654-4854
Tel: 800-621-8335
http://www.ama-assn.org

*For comprehensive information on careers in psychiatry, contact*
**American Psychiatric Association**
1000 Wilson Boulevard, Suite 1825
Arlington, VA 22209-3901
Tel: 888-357-7924
E-mail: apa@psych.org
http://www.psych.org

*To learn more about careers in medicine and how to apply to medical schools, visit the association's Web site.*
**Association of American Medical Colleges**
2450 N Street, NW
Washington, DC 20037-1126
Tel: 202-828-0400
http://www.aamc.org

*For information on mental health, and to read the newsletter* The Bell, *which contains current information about the field, visit the association's Web site.*
**Mental Health America**
2000 North Beauregard Street, 6th Floor
Alexandria, VA 22311-1748
Tel: 703-684-7722
http://www.nmha.org

*For information on mental health issues, contact*
**National Institute of Mental Health**
Science Writing, Press, and Dissemination Branch
6001 Executive Boulevard, Room 8184, MSC 9663
Bethesda, MD 20892-9663
Tel: 866-615-6464
E-mail: nimhinfo@nih.gov
http://www.nimh.nih.gov

# Psychologists

## QUICK FACTS

**School Subjects**
Biology
Psychology
Sociology

**Personal Skills**
Helping/teaching
Technical/scientific

**Work Environment**
Primarily indoors
Primarily one location

**Minimum Education Level**
Master's degree

**Salary Range**
$39,270 to $66,040 to
$109,470+

**Certification or Licensing**
Voluntary (certification)
Required for certain
positions (licensing)

**Outlook**
About as fast as the average

**DOT**
045

**GOE**
12.02.02

**NOC**
4151

**O*NET-SOC**
19-3031.00, 19-3031.01,
19-3031.02, 19-3031.03,
19-3032.00, 25-1066.00

## OVERVIEW

*Psychologists* teach, counsel, conduct research, or administer programs to understand people and help people understand themselves. Psychologists examine individual and group behavior through testing, experimenting, and studying personal histories.

Psychologists normally hold doctorates in psychology. Unlike psychiatrists, they are not medical doctors and cannot prescribe medication. Approximately 170,200 psychologists are employed in the United States.

## HISTORY

The first syllable in *psychology* derives from *psyche,* a Greek word meaning soul. The second half of *psychology* contains the root of the word *logic.* Thus, psychology translates as "the science of the soul."

Early philosophers emphasized differences between body and soul. Plato, for example, believed they were two entirely different parts. Modern scholars tend to emphasize the unity between mind and body rather than their dissimilarity.

The founder of experimental psychology, Wilhelm Wundt, held both an M.D. and a Ph.D. A physician, he taught at the University of Leipzig, where his title was professor of philosophy. Like Wundt, German scholars of the 19th century were committed to the scientific method. Discovery by experiment was considered the only respectable way for learned thinkers to work. Thus it was not thought strange that in 1879, Wundt set up an experimental laboratory to conduct research upon human behavior. Many people who later became famous psychologists in the United States received their training under Wundt.

At the turn of the 20th century, Russian physiologist Ivan Pavlov discovered a key aspect of behaviorist theory while studying the process of digestion. While experimenting on dogs, he found that they began to salivate in anticipation of their food. He discovered that if he rang a bell before presenting their meat, the dogs associated the sound of a bell with mealtime. He then would ring the bell but withhold the food. The dogs' saliva flowed anyway, whether or not they saw or smelled food. Pavlov called this substitute stimulus a "conditioned response." Many psychologists began to incorporate the theory of conditioned response into their theories of learning.

One of the most famous pioneers in psychology was Sigmund Freud, whose work led to many of the modern theories of behavior. Freud lived and practiced in Vienna, Austria, until Nazi leader Adolf Hitler's forces caused him to flee to England. His work on the meaning of dreams, the unconscious, and the nature of various emotional disturbances has had a profound effect upon the profession and practice of psychology for more than a century, although many psychologists now disagree with some of his theories.

Many Americans have contributed greatly to the science that seeks to understand human behavior: William James, Robert Woodworth, E. L. Thorndike, Clark Hull, B. F. Skinner, and others.

## THE JOB

Psychology is both a science and a profession. As a science, it is a systematic approach to the understanding of people and their behavior; as a profession, it is the application of that understanding to help solve human problems. Psychology is a rapidly growing field, and psychologists work on a great variety of problems.

The field of psychology is so vast that no one person can become an expert in all of its specialties. The psychologist usually concentrates on one specialty. Many specialists use overlapping methodologies, theories, and treatments.

Many psychologists teach some area of basic psychology in colleges and universities. They are also likely to conduct research and supervise graduate student work in an area of special interest.

*Clinical psychologists* comprise the largest group of specialists. They concern themselves with people's mental and emotional disorders. They assess and treat problems ranging from normal psychological crises, such as adolescent rebellion or middle-age loss of self-esteem, to extreme conditions, such as severe depression and schizophrenia. Areas of specialization within clinical psychology include child psychology, geropsychology, health psychology, and neuropsychology. *Child psychologists* work almost exclusively with children. They may be staff members at a child guidance clinic or a treatment center for children at a large general hospital. Child psychologists and other clinical psychologists may engage in private practice, seeing clients at offices. *Geropsychologists* specialize in treating the elderly and the special challenges they face as they age, including loss of loved ones and chronic medical conditions. *Health psychologists* help people adjust to illnesses and improve their health via counseling. *Neuropsychologists* study the link between behavior and the human brain and often are employed in head injury and stroke treatment programs.

*Developmental psychologists* study how people develop from birth through old age. They describe, measure, and explain age-related changes in behavior, stages of emotional development, universal traits and individual differences, and abnormal changes in development. Many developmental psychologists teach and do research in colleges and universities. Some specialize in programs for children in day care centers, preschools, hospitals, or clinics.

*Social psychologists* study how people interact with one other, and how individuals are affected by their environment. Social psychology has developed from four sources: sociology, cultural anthropology, psychiatry, and psychology. Social psychologists are interested in individual and group behavior. They study the ways groups influence individuals and vice versa. They study different kinds of groups: ethnic, religious, political, educational, family, and many others. The social psychologist has devised ways to research group nature, attitudes, leadership patterns, and structure.

*Counseling psychologists* work with people who have problems they find difficult to face alone. These clients are not usually mentally or emotionally ill, but they are emotionally upset, anxious, or struggling with some conflict within themselves or their environment. By helping people solve their problems, make decisions, and cope with everyday stresses, the counseling psychologist actually is working in preventive mental health.

*School psychologists* frequently do diagnosis and remediation. They may engage primarily in preventive and developmental psychology. Many school psychologists are assigned the duty of testing pupils surmised to be exceptional. Other school psychologists work almost entirely with children who have proven to be a problem to themselves or to others and who have been referred for help by teachers or other members of the school system. Many school psychologists are concerned with pupils who reveal various kinds of learning disabilities. School psychologists may also be called upon to work with relationship problems between parents and children.

*Psychometrists work* with intelligence, personality, and aptitude tests used in clinics, counseling centers, schools, and businesses. They administer tests, score them, and interpret results as related to standard norms. Psychometrists also study methods and techniques used to acquire and evaluate psychological data. They may devise new, more reliable tests. These specialists are usually well trained in mathematics, statistics, and computer programming and technology.

The *educational psychologist* is concerned primarily with how people teach, learn, and evaluate learning. Many educational psychologists are employed on college or university faculties, and they also conduct research into learning theory. Educational psychologists are also interested in the evaluation of learning.

*Experimental* or *research psychologists* conduct scientific experiments on particular aspects of behavior, either animal or human. Much experimental study is done in learning, in physiological psychology (the relationship of behavior to physiological processes), and in comparative psychology (sometimes called animal psychology). Many experimental psychological studies are carried out with animals, partly because their environments can be carefully controlled.

Other psychologists who practice outside social work-related settings include *industrial-organizational psychologists, engineering psychologists, and consumer psychologists.* Industrial-organizational psychologists are concerned with the relation between people and work. They deal with organizational structure, worker productivity, job satisfaction, consumer behavior, personnel training and development, and the interaction between humans and machines. Engineering psychologists are industrial psychologists who help engineers and technicians design systems that require workers or consumers and machines to interact. Consumer psychologists are interested in consumer reactions to products or services. These psychologists may be asked to determine the kinds of products the public will buy.

Many psychologists of all kinds find that writing skills are helpful. They may write up the results of research efforts for a scholarly journal. Psychologists prepare papers for presentation at professional association meetings and sometimes write books or articles. As consultants or industrial psychologists, they may write instruction manuals. Educational psychologists may prepare test manuals.

Some psychologists become administrators who direct college or university psychology departments or personnel services programs in a school system or industry. Some become agency or department directors of research in scientific laboratories. They may be promoted to department head in a state or federal government agency. *Chief psychologists* in hospitals or psychiatric centers plan psychological treatment programs, direct professional and nonprofessional personnel, and oversee psychological services provided by the institution.

# REQUIREMENTS

## High School

Because you will need to continue your education beyond high school in order to become a psychologist, you should enroll in college preparatory courses. Your class schedule should concentrate on English courses, computer science, mathematics, and sciences. Algebra, geometry, and calculus are important to take, as are biology, chemistry, and physics. You should take social science courses, such as psychology and sociology. You should also take a modern foreign language, such as French or German, because reading comprehension of these languages is one of the usual requirements for obtaining the doctorate degree.

## Postsecondary Training

A doctorate in psychology (Ph.D. or Psy.D.) is recommended. Some positions are available to people with a master's degree, but they are jobs of lesser responsibility and lower salaries than those open to people with a doctorate.

Psychology is an obvious choice for your college major, but not all graduate programs require entering students to have a psychology bachelor's degree. Nevertheless, your college studies should include a number of psychology courses, such as experimental psychology, developmental psychology, and abnormal psychology. You should also take classes in statistics as well as such classes as English, foreign language, and history to complete a strong liberal arts education.

Master's degree programs typically take two years to complete. Course work at this level usually involves statistics, ethics, and industrial and organizational content. If you want to work as a school psychologist, you will need to complete a supervised, yearlong internship at a school after receiving your degree.

Some doctoral programs accept students with master's degrees; in other cases, students enter a doctoral program with only a bachelor's degree. Because entrance requirements vary, you will need to research the programs you are interested in to find out their specific requirements. The doctorate degree typically takes between four and seven years to complete for those who begin their studies with only the bachelor's degree. Coursework will include studies in various areas of psychology and research (including work in quantitative research methods). Those who focus on research often complete a yearlong postdoctoral fellowship. Those who want to work as clinical, counseling, or school psychologists must complete a one-year supervised internship. Frequently those who are interested in clinical, counseling, or school psychology will get the Psy.D., because this degree emphasizes clinical rather than research work. In addition, those interested in these three areas should attend a program accredited by the American Psychological Association (APA). The National Association of School Psychologists also approves advanced degree programs in school psychology.

Unlike psychiatrists, psychologists do not need to attend medical school.

### Certification or Licensing

The American Board of Professional Psychology offers voluntary specialty certification in 13 areas, including clinical child and adolescent psychology, clinical health psychology, clinical neuropsychology, clinical psychology, cognitive and behavioral psychology, counseling psychology, couple and family psychology, forensic psychology, group psychology, organizational and business consulting psychology, psychoanalysis in psychology, rehabilitation psychology, and school psychology. Requirements for certification include having a doctorate in psychology, professional experience, appropriate postdoctoral training, and the passing of an examination. Those who fulfill these requirements receive the designation of diplomate.

The National Association of School Psychologists awards the nationally certified school psychologist designation to applicants who complete educational requirements, an internship, and pass an examination. More than 30 states recognize this designation.

Psychologists in independent practice or those providing any type of patient care, such as clinical, counseling, and school psychologists, must be licensed or certified by the state in which they practice. Some states require the licensing of industrial-organizational psychologists. Because requirements vary, you will need to check with your state's licensing board for specific information.

### Other Requirements

Because psychology is such a broad field, various personal attributes apply to different psychology positions. Those involved in research, for example, should be analytical, detail oriented, and have strong math and writing skills. Those working with patients should be "people persons," able to relate to others, and have excellent listening skills. No matter what their area of focus, however, all psychologists should be committed to lifelong learning since our understanding of humans is constantly evolving.

To be a psychologist, one must have a desire to help people understand themselves and others. A basic curiosity is required as well as a fascination with the way the human mind works.

## EXPLORING

If you are interested in psychology, explore the field by taking psychology classes in high school and reading all you can about the subject, including biographies of and works by noted psychologists. In addition, make an appointment to talk about the profession with a psychologist who may work at a nearby school, college, hospital, or clinic. Use the Internet to learn more about mental health issues by visiting Web sites, such as that of Mental Health America at http://www.nmha.org or the APA at http://www.apa.org.

If being involved with patient care interests you, gain experience in the health care field by volunteering at a local hospital or clinic. In addition, volunteer opportunities may exist at local nursing homes, where you will also have the chance to work with clients needing some type of assistance. If doing research work sounds appealing to you, consider joining your school's science club, which may offer the opportunity to work on projects, document the process, and work as part of a team.

## EMPLOYERS

Approximately 170,200 psychologists are employed in the United States. Clinical psychologists may teach at colleges or universities. Or, clinical psychologists may work with patients in a private practice or a hospital, where they provide therapy after evaluation through special tests.

Many developmental psychologists teach and research in colleges and universities. Some specialize in programs for children in day care centers, preschools, hospitals, or clinics. About 34 percent of psychologists are self-employed.

Social psychologists often teach and conduct research in colleges or universities. They also work for agencies of the federal or state government or in private research firms. Some work as consultants. An increasing number of social psychologists work as researchers and personnel managers in such nontraditional settings as advertising agencies, corporations, and architectural and engineering firms.

Counseling psychologists work in college or university counseling centers; they also teach in psychology departments. They may be in private practice. Or they may work at a community health center, a marriage counseling agency, or a federal agency such as the Department of Veterans Affairs.

## STARTING OUT

Those entering the field with only a bachelor's degree will face strong competition for few jobs. The university career services office or a psychology professor may be able to help such a student find a position assisting a psychologist at a health center or other location. Positions beyond the assistant level, however, will be very difficult to attain. Those graduating from master's or doctorate degree programs will find more employment opportunities. Again, university career services offices may be able to provide these graduates with assistance. In addition, contacts made during an internship may offer job leads. Joining professional organizations and networking with members is also a way to find out about job openings. These organizations, such as the APA, often list job vacancies in their publications for members.

## ADVANCEMENT

For those who have bachelor's or master's degrees, the first step to professional advancement is to complete a doctorate degree. After that, advancement will depend on the area of psychology in which the person is working. For example, a psychologist teaching at a college or university may advance through the academic ranks from instructor to professor. Some college teachers who enjoy administrative work become department heads.

Psychologists who work for state or federal government agencies may, after considerable experience, be promoted to head a section or department. School psychologists might become directors of pupil personnel services. Industrial psychologists can rise to managerial or administrative positions.

After several years of experience, many psychologists enter private practice or set up their own research or consulting firms.

## EARNINGS

Because the psychology field offers so many different types of employment possibilities, salaries for psychologists vary greatly. In addition, the typical conditions affecting salaries, such as the person's level of education, professional experience, and location, also apply. The U.S. Department of Labor reports that clinical, counseling, and school psychologists earned median salaries of $66,040 in 2009. Salaries ranged from less than $39,270 to $109,470 or more. The department also reports the following mean annual earnings for clinical, counseling, and school psychologists by employer: offices of other health practitioners, $87,270; psychiatric and substance abuse hospitals, $83,120; elementary/secondary schools, $69,870; individual and family services, $70,490; and outpatient care centers, $69,620.

Benefits for full-time workers include vacation and sick time, health, and sometimes dental, insurance, and pension or 401(k) plans. Self-employed psychologists must provide their own benefits.

## WORK ENVIRONMENT

Psychologists work under many different conditions. Those who work as college or university teachers usually have offices in a building on campus and access to a laboratory in which they carry out experiments.

Offices of school psychologists may be located in the school system headquarters. They may see students and their parents at those offices, or they might work in space set aside for them in several schools within the school district that they may visit regularly.

Psychologists in military service serve in the United States or overseas. They may be stationed in Washington, D.C., and assigned to an office job, or they may be stationed with other military personnel at a post or, more likely, in a military hospital.

Psychologists employed in government work in such diverse places as public health or vocational rehabilitation agencies, the Department of Veterans Affairs, the Peace Corps, the U.S. Department of Education, or a state department of education. Their working conditions depend largely on the kind of jobs they have. They may be required to travel or to write and publish papers. They may work directly with people or be assigned entirely to research.

Some psychologists are self-employed. Most work as clinical psychologists and have offices where they see clients individually. Others work as consultants to business firms. Self-employed psychologists rent or own their office spaces and arrange their own work schedules.

## OUTLOOK

The U.S. Department of Labor projects that employment for psychologists will grow about as fast as the average for all occupations through 2018, with the largest increase in schools, hospitals, social service agencies, consulting firms, mental health centers, substance abuse treatment clinics, and private companies. Increased emphasis on health maintenance and illness prevention as well as growing interest in psychological services for special groups, such as children, the elderly, substance abusers, or returning military veterans, will create demand for psychologists. Many of these areas depend on government funding, however, and could be adversely affected in an economic downswing when spending is likely to be curtailed. Many openings should be available in business and industry, and the outlook is very good for psychologists who are in full-time independent practice.

Prospects look best for those with doctorates in applied areas, such as clinical, counseling, health, industrial/organizational, and school psychology, and for those with extensive technical training in quantitative research methods and computer applications. Postdoctorates are becoming increasingly crucial in the fields of research psychology that deal with behavior based on biology.

Competition for jobs will be tougher for those with master's (except in industrial-organizational psychology, which will experience much-faster-than-average growth) or bachelor's degrees. Most job candidates with bachelor's degrees, in fact, will not be able to find employment in the psychology field beyond assistant-level jobs at such places as rehabilitation centers. Some may work as high school psychology teachers if they meet state teaching certification requirements.

## FOR MORE INFORMATION

*For information on specialty certification, contact*
American Board of Professional Psychology
600 Market Street, Suite 300
Chapel Hill, NC 27516-4057
Tel: 919-537-8031
E-mail: office@abpp.org
http://www.abpp.org

*For more on careers in psychology and mental health issues, contact*
American Psychological Association
750 First Street, NE
Washington, DC 20002-4242
Tel: 800-374-2721
http://www.apa.org

*For licensing information, visit the following Web site:*
**Association of State and Provincial Psychology Boards**
PO Box 241245
Montgomery, AL 36124-1245
Tel: 334-832-4580
E-mail: asppb@asppb.org
http://www.asppb.org

*For more information on certification and becoming a school psychologist, including graduate school information, contact*
**National Association of School Psychologists**
4340 East-West Highway, Suite 402
Bethesda, MD 20814-4468
Tel: 866-331-6277
E-mail: nasp@nasweb.org
http://www.nasponline.org

*For a list of Canadian psychology departments providing graduate programs, contact*
**Canadian Psychological Association**
141 Laurier Avenue West, Suite 702
Ottawa, ON K1P 5J3 Canada
Tel: 613-237-2144
E-mail: cpa@cpa.ca
http://www.cpa.ca

*For a whimsical introduction to psychology, visit*
**ePsych**
http://epsych.msstate.edu

# Recreational Therapists

## OVERVIEW

*Recreational therapists,* also known as *therapeutic recreation specialists,* plan, organize, direct, and monitor medically approved recreation programs for patients in hospitals, clinics, and various community settings. These therapists use recreational activities to assist patients with mental, physical, or emotional disabilities to achieve the maximum possible functional independence. Recreational therapists hold approximately 23,300 jobs in the United States.

## HISTORY

The field of therapy has expanded in the past few decades to include recreational therapy as a form of medical treatment. Its use grew out of the realization that soldiers suffering from battle fatigue, shock, and emotional trauma respond positively to organized recreation and activity programs.

As a result, therapy for people in nursing homes, hospitals, mental institutions, and adult care facilities is no longer limited to physical therapy. Experiments have shown that recovery is aided by recreational activities such as sports, music, art, gardening, dance, drama, field trips, and other pastimes. Elderly people are more healthy and alert when their days are filled with activities, field trips, and social get-togethers. People with disabilities can gain greater self-confidence and awareness of their own abilities when they get involved with sports, crafts, and other activities. People recovering from drug or alcohol addiction can reaffirm their self-worth through directed hobbies, clubs, and sports. The recreational therapist is a health professional who organizes these types of activities and helps patients take an active role in their own recovery.

## THE JOB

Recreational therapists work with people who are mentally, physically, or emotionally disabled. They are professionals who employ leisure activities as a form of treatment, much as other health practitioners use surgery, drugs, nutrition, exercise, or psychotherapy. Recreational therapists strive to minimize patients' symptoms, restore function, and improve their physical, mental, and emotional well-being. Enhancing the patient's ability to take part in everyday life is the primary goal of recreational therapy; interesting and rewarding activities are the means for working toward that goal.

Recreational therapists work in a number of different settings, including nursing homes, adult day care programs, mental hospitals, outpatient facilities, community mental health centers, residential facilities for the mentally disabled, school systems, and prisons. They can work as individual staff members, as independent consultants, or as part of a larger therapeutic team. They may get personally involved with patients or direct the work of assistants and support staff.

The recreational therapist first confers with the doctors, psychiatrists, social workers, physical therapists, and other professionals on staff to coordinate their efforts in treatment. The recreational therapist needs to understand the nature of the patient's ailment, current physical and mental capacities, emotional state, and prospects for recovery. The patient's family and friends are also consulted to find out the patient's interests and hobbies. With this information, the recreational therapist then plans an agenda of activities for that person.

To enrich the lives of people in hospitals and other institutions, recreational therapists use imagination and skill in organizing beneficial activities. Sports, games, arts and crafts, movie screenings, field trips, hobby clubs, and dramatics are only a few examples of activities that can enrich the lives of patients. Some therapists specialize in certain areas. *Dance/movement therapists* plan and conduct dance and body movement exercises to improve patients' physical and mental well-being. *Art therapists* work with patients in various art methods, such as drawing, painting, and ceramics, as part of their therapeutic and recovery programs. Therapists may also work with pets and other animals, such as horses. *Music therapists* design programs for patients that can involve solo or group singing, playing in bands, rhythmic and other creative activities, listening to music, or attending concerts. Even flowers and gardening can prove beneficial to patients, as is proved by the work of *horticultural therapists.* When the treatment team feels that regular employment would help certain patients, the *industrial therapist* arranges a productive job for the patient in an actual work environment, one that will have the greatest therapeutic value based on the patient's needs and abilities. *Orientation therapists* for the blind work with people who have recently lost their sight, helping them to readjust to daily living and independence through training and exercise. All of these professional therapists plan their programs to meet the needs and capabilities of patients. They also carefully monitor and record each patient's progress and report it to the other members of the medical team.

As part of their jobs, recreational therapists need to understand their patients and set goals for their progress accordingly. A patient having trouble socializing, for example, may have an interest in playing chess but be overwhelmed by the prospect of actually playing, since that involves interaction with another person. A therapist would proceed slowly, first letting the patient observe a number of games and then assigning a therapeutic assistant to serve as a chess partner for weeks or even months, as long as it takes for the patient to gain enough confidence to seek out other patients for chess partners. The therapist makes a note of the patient's response, modifies the therapy program accordingly, and lets other professionals know of the results. If a patient responds more enthusiastically to the program, works more cooperatively with others, or becomes more disruptive, the therapist must note these reactions and periodically reevaluate the patient's activity program.

Responsibilities and elements of the job can vary, depending on the setting in which the recreational therapist works. In nursing homes, the therapist often groups residents according to common or shared interests and ability levels and then plans field trips, parties, entertainment, and other group activities. The therapist documents residents' responses to the activities and continually searches for ways of heightening residents' enjoyment of recreational and leisure activities, not just in the facility but in the surrounding community as well. Because nursing home residents are likely to remain in the facility for months or even years, the activities program makes a big difference in the quality of their lives. Without the stimulation of interesting events to look forward to and participate in, the daily routine of a nursing home can become monotonous and depressing, and some residents are apt to deteriorate both mentally and physically. In some nursing homes, recreational therapists direct the activities program. In others, activities coordinators plan and carry out the program under the part-time supervision of a consultant who is either a recreational or occupational therapist.

The therapist in a community center might work in a day care program for the elderly or in a program for mentally disabled adults operated by a county recreation department. No matter what the disability, recreational therapists in community settings face the added logistical challenge of arranging transportation and supervision, if necessary, for prospective participants. Coordinating transportation is less of a problem in hospitals and nursing homes, where the patients all live under one roof. Developing therapeutic recreation programs in community settings requires a large measure of organizational ability, flexibility, and ingenuity.

## REQUIREMENTS

### High School

You can prepare for a career as a recreational therapist by taking your high school's college preparatory program. Naturally, this should include science classes, such as biology and chemistry, as well as mathematics and history classes. You can begin to gain an understanding of human behavior by taking psychology and sociology classes. For exposure to a variety of recreation specialties, take physical education, art, music, and drama classes. Verbal and written communication skills are essential for this work, so take English and speech classes. This job will require you to write reports, so computer science skills are also essential.

### Postsecondary Training

More than 100 recreational therapy programs, which offer degrees ranging from the associate to the doctoral level, are currently available in the United States. While associate degrees in recreational therapy exist, such a degree will allow you only to work at the paraprofessional level. To be eligible for an entry-level professional position as a recreational therapist, you will need a bachelor's degree. Acceptable majors are recreational therapy, therapeutic recreation, and recreation with a concentration in therapeutic recreation. A typical four-year bachelor's degree program includes courses in both natural science (such as biology, behavioral science, and human anatomy) and social science (such as psychology and sociology). Courses more specific to the profession include programming for special populations (such as the elderly); rehabilitative techniques including self-help skills, mobility, signing for the deaf, and orientation for the blind; medical equipment; current treatment approaches; legal issues; and professional ethics. In addition, you will need to complete a supervised internship or field placement lasting a minimum of 480 hours.

Continuing education is increasingly becoming a requirement for professionals in this field. Many therapists attend conferences and seminars and take additional university courses. A number of professional organizations (for example, the National Therapeutic Recreation Society and the American Therapeutic Recreation Association) offer continuing education opportunities. Those with degrees in related fields can enter the profession by earning master's degrees in therapeutic recreation or recreational therapy. Advanced degrees are recommended for those seeking advancement to supervisory, administrative, and teaching positions. These requirements will become more strict as more professionals enter the field.

## Certification or Licensing

A number of states regulate the profession of therapeutic recreation. Licensing is required in some states; professional certification (or eligibility for certification) is required in others; titling is regulated in some states and at some facilities. In other states, many hospitals and other employers require recreational therapists to be certified. Certification is recommended for recreational therapists as a way to show professional accomplishment. It is available through the National Council for Therapeutic Recreation Certification. To receive certification you must meet eligibility requirements, including education and experience, as well as pass an exam. You are then given the title of certified therapeutic recreation specialist. Because of the variety of certification and licensing requirements, you must check with both your state and your employer for specific information on your situation. Most clinical settings require therapists to be certified.

## Other Requirements

To be a successful recreational therapist, you must enjoy and be enthusiastic about the activities in which you involve your clients. You will also need patience and a positive attitude. Since this is people-oriented work, therapists must be able to relate to many different people in a variety of settings. They must be able to deal assertively and politely with other health care workers, such as doctors and nurses, as well as with the clients themselves and their families. In addition, successful therapists must be creative and have strong communication skills in order to develop and explain activities to patients.

# EXPLORING

If you are interested in recreational therapy, you can find part-time or summer work as a sports coach or referee, park supervisor, or camp counselor. Volunteer work in a nursing home, hospital, or care facility for disabled adults is also a good way to learn about the daily realities of institutional living. These types of facilities are always looking for volunteers to work with and visit patients. Working with people with physical, mental, or emotional disabilities can be stressful, and volunteer work is a good way for you to test whether you can handle this kind of stress.

## EMPLOYERS

Recreational therapists hold approximately 23,300 jobs, according to the U.S. Department of Labor. Many of these jobs are in nursing and residential care facilities and hospitals. Other employers include adult day care centers and substance abuse centers, and some therapists are self-employed. Employment opportunities also exist in long-term rehabilitation, home health care, correctional facilities, psychiatric facilities, and transitional programs.

## STARTING OUT

There are many methods for finding out about available jobs in recreational therapy. A good place to start is the job notices and want ads printed in the local newspapers, bulletins from state park and recreation societies, and publications of the professional associations previously mentioned. State employment agencies and human service departments will know of job openings in state hospitals. College career services offices might also be able to put new recreational therapy graduates in touch with prospective employers. Internship programs are sometimes available, offering good opportunities to find potential full-time jobs.

Recent graduates should also make appointments to meet potential employers personally. Most colleges and universities offer career counseling services. Most employers will make themselves available to discuss their programs and the possibility of hiring extra staff. They may also guide new graduates to other institutions currently hiring therapists. Joining professional associations, both state and national, and attending conferences are good ways to meet potential employers and colleagues.

## ADVANCEMENT

Newly graduated recreational therapists generally begin as *staff therapists*. Advancement is chiefly to supervisory or administrative positions, usually after some years of experience and continuing education. Some therapists teach, conduct research, or do consulting work on a contract basis; a graduate degree is essential for moving into these areas.

Many therapists continue their education but prefer to continue working with patients. For variety, they may choose to work with new groups of people or get a job in a new setting, such as moving from a facility for the disabled to a retirement home. Some may also move to a related field, such as special education, or sales positions involving products and services related to recreational therapy.

## EARNINGS

Salaries of recreational therapists vary according to educational background, experience, certification, and region of the country. Recreational therapists had median earnings of $39,440 in 2009, according to the U.S. Department of Labor. The lowest paid 10 percent earned less than $24,510 a year, while the highest paid 10 percent earned more than $62,170 annually. Employment setting is also an important factor in determining salary. Recreational therapists employed by nursing care facilities earned mean incomes of $36,210, while those employed by general medical and surgical hospitals earned $44,840. Those in management positions command higher salaries. Salaries for supervisors range from $50,000 to $75,000 or more annually; and some consultants and educators reported even higher earnings.

Therapists employed at hospitals, clinics, and other facilities generally enjoy a full benefits package, including health insurance and vacation, holiday, and sick pay. Consultants and self-employed therapists must provide their own benefits.

## WORK ENVIRONMENT

Working conditions vary, but recreational therapists generally work in a ward, a specially equipped activity room, or at a nursing home. In a community setting, recreational therapists may interview subjects and plan activities in an office, but they might work in a gymnasium, swimming pool, playground, or outdoors on a nature walk when leading activities. Therapists may also work on horse ranches, farms, and other outdoor facilities catering to people with disabilities.

The job may be physically tiring because therapists are often on their feet all day and may have to lift and carry equipment. Recreational therapists generally work a standard 40-hour week, although weekend and evening hours may be required. Supervisors may have to work overtime, depending on their workload.

## OUTLOOK

The U.S. Department of Labor predicts that employment for recreational therapists will grow faster than the average for all occupations through 2018. Employment in nursing homes will grow faster than in other areas. Fast employment growth is expected in assisted living, outpatient physical and psychiatric rehabilitation, and services for people with disabilities. Increased life expectancies for the elderly and for people with developmental disabilities such as Down syndrome will create opportunities for recreational therapists. The incidence of alcohol and drug dependency problems is also growing, creating a demand for qualified therapists to work in short-term alcohol and drug abuse clinics. There will also be new opportunities in schools as a result of growing enrollments and increased federal funding of services for students with disabilities.

Most openings for recreational therapists will be in health care and assisted living facilities because of the increasing numbers and greater longevity of the elderly. There is also greater public pressure to regulate and improve the quality of life in retirement centers, which may mean more jobs and increased scrutiny of recreational therapists.

Growth in hospital jobs is not expected to be great. Many of the new jobs created will be in hospital-based adult day care programs or in units offering short-term mental health services. Because of economic and social factors, little growth is expected in public mental hospitals. Many of the programs and services formerly offered there are being shifted to community residential facilities for the disabled. Community programs for special populations are expected to expand significantly.

## FOR MORE INFORMATION

*For career information and resources, contact*
**American Association for Physical Activity and Recreation**
1900 Association Drive
Reston, VA 20191-1598
Tel: 703-476-3430
E-mail: aapar@aahperd.org
http://www.aahperd.org/aapar

*For career information, a list of colleges and universities that offer training, and job listings, contact*
**American Therapeutic Recreation Association**
629 North Main Street

Hattiesburg, MS 39401-3429
Tel: 601-450-2872
http://www.atra-online.com

*For information on certification, contact*
**National Council for Therapeutic Recreation Certification**
7 Elmwood Drive
New City, NY 10956-5136
Tel: 845-639-1439
E-mail: nctrc@nctrc.org
http://www.nctrc.org

*For career information, contact*
**National Therapeutic Recreation Society**
22377 Belmont Ridge Road
Ashburn, VA 20148-4501
Tel: 800-626-6772
http://www.nrpa.org/ntrs

*Visit this Web site to find out about jobs, activities, schools, and other information related to the field.*
**Therapeutic Recreation Directory**
http://www.recreationtherapy.com

---

## INTERVIEW

*Dr. Mary Ann Aquadro is the president-elect of the American Therapeutic Recreation Association. She discussed her career and the field of recreational therapy with the editors of* Careers in Focus: Social Work.

**Q. Can you tell us about your professional background?**

**A.** I completed my bachelor of science degree in park and recreation administration with emphasis in therapeutic recreation at the University of Memphis in December 1980. Shortly after graduation, in January 1981, I became employed by the Veterans Administration Medical Center in Murfreesboro, Tennessee, as a recreation therapist. For the next seven years I worked with substance abuse rehabilitation patients on short-term and residential units and with long-term care patients. I earned and have maintained the national credential of certified therapeutic recreation specialist. In 1988, I was promoted to chief, recreation therapy at the Murfreesboro Veterans Administration

Medical Center, and have worked in that position for the last 21 years. I supervise a staff of recreation therapists and recreation therapy assistants and manage the department, which has employed as many as 18 therapists and assistants. I have been an active member of the national professional association, The American Therapeutic Recreation Association, for more than 20 years. Throughout this time I continued my education at Middle Tennessee State University (MTSU). I completed my master of science degree in 1989 and my Ph.D. in 2008. I have taught recreation therapy courses at MTSU as an adjunct faculty member.

**Q. What made you want to enter this career?**

**A.** I attended Immaculate Conception High School in Memphis, Tennessee. The students were encouraged to perform volunteer work and, by choice, I always seemed to perform my volunteer work in facilities that treated individuals with disabilities. I thoroughly enjoyed interacting with these individuals and bringing some much-appreciated happiness to them. Throughout my childhood I was always athletic and enjoyed many types of recreational activities. Finding a profession that allowed me to interact and assist individuals with disabling conditions through enjoyable recreational activities was a natural transition from being a student to a professional.

**Q. What is one thing people may not know about a career in therapeutic recreation?**

**A.** Qualified providers of recreational therapy are nationally certified by the National Council for Therapeutic Recreation Certification.

Recreational therapy plays a critical role in the comprehensive rehabilitation of individuals with disabling conditions by contributing to the broad spectrum of health care through delivery of treatment services and through recreational activities—each of which is instrumental in improving and maintaining physical and psychosocial functioning, preventing secondary health conditions, and enhancing independent living skills and overall quality of life.

There are recreational therapists employed in a tremendous variety of health care settings, and they work with numerous patient populations. The health care settings include hospitals, schools, nursing homes, physical rehabilitation facilities, mental health facilities, prisons, community recreation departments, home health, and others. These populations include all ages—from pediatrics to geriatrics. They include diagnoses such as traumatic brain injury, mental health disorders, physical disabilities, developmental disabilities, substance abuse, at risk youth, terminally ill, Alzheimer's disease and other dementias, visual impairment, and many others. The settings and populations are very diverse.

Q. **What are the most important personal and professional qualities for recreational therapists?**

A. Important personal qualities include the desire to work closely with individuals with disabling illnesses and conditions, leadership skills, patience, organizational skills but also the ability to be flexible, take initiative, and be creative. Due to the variety of physical, cognitive, emotional, and social limitations of the patients/clients with whom we work, it is necessary to be the professional leader in individual and group interventions. Patience is necessary because their limitations often require repetitiveness and progress is often very slow and sometimes does not occur at all. Organizational skills are critical because of the number of patients/clients we treat, planning the treatments in advance based on the needs of the patients/clients, and the administrative duties required such as documentation in medical records, securing needed supplies, attendance at required meetings, etc. However, although organization is extremely important, flexibility is equally as important due to the special needs of the patients/clients and because plans must often be altered based on these needs. Initiative and creativity are critical because recreational therapists work independently to assess the needs of their patients/clients and implement the needed interventions. You must be self-motivated to provide the most effective treatment possible and, due to the variation in the needs of their patients/clients, must often be very creative when addressing these needs.

Professionally, it is important to stay abreast of knowledge related to your profession; work closely with other treatment team members; be compassionate, yet professional, when working with your patient/clients; and be dedicated to your profession. Being a recreational therapist is more than having a job . . . it is being a professional health care provider.

Q. **What advice would you give to young people who want to enter the field?**

A. I would recommend performing volunteer work in as many facilities and with as many patient populations as possible while in high school and in college to [gain] experience and to discover which population(s) really interests you. The experience gives you "an edge" when applying for your first position after graduation. It is often necessary to be very open-minded when seeking employment in your first position after graduation and it may not be the exact type of position you desire. However, it is much easier to find a more preferable position if you are currently employed. This is true in any profession. Through experience between the volunteer work and employment, eventually you will be able to become employed in a position that is [. . .] enjoyable and with increased salary and leads to a rewarding career.

**Q. What are the benefits of membership in the American Therapeutic Recreation Association?**

**A.** The two most important benefits are the opportunities to network with other recreational therapy professionals across the country and the continuing education offered by the association. It is so important to network and learn about treatments and programs that are being offered and proven to be effective. Just as in any health care career, new interventions are constantly being developed as new knowledge regarding health care is developed. Being a member of a national professional association allows the use of resources provided by the association and allows opportunities to attend local, statewide, regional, and national workshops and conferences. At these workshops and conferences there are tremendous opportunities to network with other professionals and attend educational sessions. There are also resources provided by the association through the Web site, http://www.atra-online.com, and publications offered by the association.

**Q. How important is membership to career success?**

**A.** Staying current with new knowledge in any health care profession is critical. The opportunity for knowledge is available through membership in a professional association. Also, career opportunities often arise from individuals with whom you have made personal professional contact. There are a tremendous amount of specialties when working in health care. As you work in your profession you naturally develop a special interest in a specialty area of treatment. Networking allows you to meet and learn from other professionals who have this same interest and area of expertise. You become known for your expertise in this treatment area. When opportunities arise you may be contacted or recommended for the position due to your known expertise in that area.

# Social Workers

## OVERVIEW

*Social workers* help people and assist communities in solving problems. These problems include poverty, racism, discrimination, physical and mental illness, addiction, and abuse. They counsel individuals and families, they lead group sessions, they research social problems, and they develop policy and programs. Social workers are dedicated to empowering people and helping them to preserve their dignity and worth. Approximately 642,000 social workers are employed in the United States.

## HISTORY

Even before the United States became a country, poverty and unemployment were among society's problems. Almshouses and shelters that provided the homeless with jobs and rooms were established as early as 1657. The social work profession as we know it today, however, has its origins in the "friendly visitor" of the early 1800s; these charity workers went from home to home offering guidance in how to move beyond the troubles of poverty.

At a time when not much financial assistance was available from local governments, the poor relied on friendly visitors for instruction on household budgeting and educating their children. Despite their good intentions, however, the friendly visitors could not provide the poor with all the necessary support. The middle-class women who served as friendly visitors were generally far removed from the experiences of the lower classes. Most of the friendly visitors served the community for only a very short time and therefore did not have the opportunity to gain much experience with the poor. The great difference between

## QUICK FACTS

**School Subjects**
Health
Psychology

**Personal Skills**
Communication/ideas
Helping/teaching

**Work Environment**
Primarily indoors
Primarily multiple locations

**Minimum Education Level**
Bachelor's degree

**Salary Range**
$24,940 to $46,340 to $71,190+

**Certification or Licensing**
Required by all states

**Outlook**
Faster than the average

**DOT**
195

**GOE**
12.02.02

**NOC**
4152

**O*NET-SOC**
21-1021.00, 21-1022.00, 21-1023.00, 21-1029.00

the life experiences of the friendly visitors and the experiences of their clients sometimes resulted in serious problems: The self-esteem and ambitions of the poor were sometimes damaged by the moral judgments of the friendly visitors. In some cases, friendly visitors served only to promote their middle-class values and practices. By the late 1800s, many charitable organizations developed in U.S. and Canadian cities. With the development of these organizations came a deeper insight into improving the conditions of the poor. Serving as a friendly visitor came to be considered an apprenticeship; it became necessary for friendly visitors to build better relationships with their clients. Friendly visitors were encouraged to take the time to learn about their clients and to develop an understanding of each client's individual needs. Nevertheless, some sense of moral superiority remained, as these charitable organizations refused assistance to alcoholics, beggars, and prostitutes.

The birth of the settlement house brought charity workers even closer to their clients. Settlement houses served as communities for the poor and were staffed by young, well-educated idealists eager to solve society's problems. The staff people lived among their clients and learned from them. In 1889, Jane Addams established the best known of the settlement houses, a community in Chicago called Hull-House. Addams wrote extensively about the problems of the poor, and her efforts to provide solutions to their problems led to the foundation of social work education. She emphasized the importance of an education specific to the concerns of the social worker. By the 1920s, social work master's degree programs were established in many universities.

## Books to Read

Doelling, Carol Nesslein. *Social Work Career Development: A Handbook for Job Hunting and Career Planning.* 2d ed. Washington, D.C.: NASW Press, 2005.

Grobman, Linda May. *Days In The Lives Of Social Workers: 54 Professionals Tell "Real-Life" Stories From Social Work Practice.* 3d ed. Harrisburg, Pa.: White Hat Communications, 2004.

Ritter, Jessica, Halaevalu F. Vakalahi, and Mary Kiernan-Stern. *101 Careers in Social Work.* New York: Springer Publishing Company, 2008.

Rosenberg, Jessica. *Working in Social Work: The Real World Guide to Practice Settings.* New York: Routledge, 2009.

Wright, Natalie. *Vault Career Guide to Social Work.* New York: Vault Inc., 2008.

Theories and methodologies of social work have changed over the years, but the basis of the profession has remained the same: helping people and addressing social problems. As society changes, so do its problems, calling for redefinition of the social work profession. The first three fields of formal social work were defined by setting: medical social work, psychiatric social work, and child welfare. Later, practice was classified by different methodologies: casework, group work, and community organization. Most recently, the social work profession has been divided into two areas—direct practice and indirect practice.

## THE JOB

After months of physical abuse from her husband, a young woman has taken her children and moved out of her house. With no job and no home, and fearing for her safety, she looks for a temporary shelter for herself and her children. Once there, she can rely on the help of social workers who will provide her with a room, food, and security. The social workers will offer counseling and emotional support to help her address the problems in her life. They will involve her in group sessions with other victims of abuse. They will direct her to job training programs and other employment services. They will set up interviews with managers of low-income housing. As the woman makes efforts to improve her life, the shelter will provide day care for the children. All these resources exist because the social work profession has long been committed to empowering people and improving society.

The social worker's role extends even beyond the shelter. If the woman has trouble getting help from other agencies, the social worker will serve as an advocate, stepping in to ensure that she gets the aid to which she is entitled. The woman may also qualify for long-term assistance from the shelter, such as a second-step program in which a social worker offers counseling and other support over several months. The woman's individual experience will also help in the social worker's research of the problem of domestic violence; with that research, the social worker can help the community come to a better understanding of the problem and can direct society toward solutions. Some of these solutions may include the development of special police procedures for domestic disputes, or court-ordered therapy groups for abusive spouses.

Direct social work practice is also known as clinical practice. As the name suggests, direct practice involves working directly with the client by offering counseling, advocacy, information and referral, and education. Indirect practice concerns the structures through which the direct practice is offered. Indirect practice (a practice consisting mostly of social workers with Ph.D. degrees) involves program development and evaluation, administration, and policy analysis. The vast majority of the 150,000 members of the National Association of Social Workers (NASW) work in direct service roles.

Because of the number of problems facing individuals, families and communities, social workers find jobs in a wide variety of settings and with a variety of client groups. Some of these areas are discussed in the following paragraphs.

Health/mental health care. Mental health care has become one of the leading areas of social work employment. These jobs are competitive and typically go to more experienced social workers. Settings include community mental health centers, where social workers serve persistently mentally ill people and participate in outreach services; state and county mental hospitals, for long-term, inpatient care; facilities of the Department of Veterans Affairs, involving a variety of mental health care programs for veterans; and private psychiatric hospitals, for patients who can pay directly. Social workers also work with patients who have physical illnesses. They help individuals and their families adjust to the illness and the changes that illness may bring to their lives. They confer with physicians and with other members of the medical team to make plans about the best way to help the patient. They explain the treatment and its anticipated outcome to both the patient and the family. They help the patient adjust to the possible prospect of long hospitalization and isolation from the family.

Child care/family services. Efforts are being made to offer a more universal system of care that would incorporate child care, family services, and community service. Child care services include day care homes, child care centers, and Head Start centers. Social workers in these settings attempt to address all the problems children face from infancy to late adolescence. They work with families to detect problems early and intervene when necessary. They research the problems confronting children and families, and they establish new services or adapt existing services to address these problems. They provide parenting education to teenage parents, which can involve living with a teenage parent in a foster care situation, teaching parenting skills, and caring for the baby while the parent attends school. Social workers alert employers to employees' needs for daytime child care.

Social workers in this area of service are constantly required to address new issues. In recent years, for example, social workers have developed services for families composed of different cultural backgrounds, services for children with congenital disabilities resulting from the mother's drug use, and disabilities related to HIV or AIDS.

A social worker counsels a group of children about their problems with moving to a new school. *(Jon Way, AP Photo)*

**Geriatric social work.** Within this field, social workers provide individual and family counseling services in order to assess the older person's needs and strengths. Social workers help older people locate transportation and housing services. They also offer adult day care services, or adult foster care services that match older people with families. Adult protective services protect older people from abuse and neglect, and respite services allow family members time off from the care of an older person. A little-recognized problem is the rising incidence of HIV/AIDS among the elderly; in 2005, 24 percent of all HIV/AIDS patients were aged 50 or over.

**School social work.** In schools, social workers serve students and their families, teachers, administrators, and other school staff members. Education, counseling, and advocacy are important aspects of school social work. With education, social workers attempt to prevent alcohol and drug abuse, teen pregnancy, and the spread of HIV/AIDS and other sexually transmitted diseases. They provide multicultural and family life education. They counsel students who are discriminated against because of their sexual orientation or racial, ethnic, or religious background. They also serve as advocates for these students, bringing issues of discrimination before administrators, school boards, and student councils.

A smaller number of social workers are employed in the areas of social work education (a field composed of the professors and instructors who teach and train students of social work); group practice (in which social workers facilitate treatment and support groups); and corrections (providing services to inmates in penal institutions). Social workers also offer counseling, occupational assistance, and advocacy to those with addictions and disabilities, to the homeless, and to women, children, and the elderly who have been in abusive situations.

Client groups expand and change as societal problems change. Social work professionals must remain aware of the problems affecting individuals and communities in order to offer assistance to as many people as possible.

Computers have become important tools for social workers. Client records are maintained on computers, allowing for easier collection and analysis of data. Interactive computer programs are used to train social workers, as well as to analyze case histories (such as for an individual's risk of HIV infection).

## REQUIREMENTS

### High School

To prepare for a social work career, you should take courses in high school that will improve your communications skills, such as English, speech, and composition. On a debate team, you could further develop your skills in communication as well as research and analysis. History, social studies, and sociology courses are important in understanding the concerns and issues of society. Although some work is available for those with only a high school diploma or associate's degree (as a social work aide or social services technician), the most opportunities exist for people with degrees in social work.

### Postsecondary Training

A minimum of a bachelor's degree in social work, psychology, sociology, or a related field is required for employment as a social worker, although many employers now require applicants to have a master's degree. The Council on Social Work Education, which accredits bachelor's and master's programs in social work, has approved 468 programs granting the bachelor's degree in social work (B.S.W.) and 196 programs granting the master's degree (M.S.W.). The council offers a listing of member programs at its Web site, http://www. cswe.org. The Group for the Advancement of Doctoral Education in Social Work (http://www.gadephd.org) provides contact information for 74 programs that offer the doctor of social work (D.S.W.) degree or the Ph.D. in social work. The Council on Social Work Education requires that five areas be covered in accredited bachelor's degree social work programs: human behavior and the social environment; social welfare policy and services; social work practice; research; and field practicum. Most programs require two years of liberal arts study followed by two years of study in the social work major. Also, students must complete a field practicum of at least 400 hours. Graduates of these programs can find work in public assistance or they can work with the elderly or with people with mental or developmental disabilities.

Although no clear lines of classification are drawn in the social work profession, most supervisory and administrative positions require at least an M.S.W. degree. Master's programs are organized according to fields of practice (such as mental health care), problem areas (substance abuse), population groups (the elderly), and practice roles (practice with individuals, families, or communities). They are usually two-year programs that require at least 900 hours of field practice. Most positions in mental health care facilities require an M.S.W. Doctoral degrees are also available and prepare students for research and teaching. Most social workers with doctorates go to work in community organizations.

### Certification or Licensing

Licensing, certification, or registration of social workers is required by all states. To receive the necessary licensing, a social worker will typically have to gain a certain amount of experience and also pass an exam. The certification programs help to identify those social workers who have gained the knowledge and experience necessary to meet national standards.

The National Association of Social Workers offers three voluntary credentials and 12 specialty certifications (eight for M.S.W.s and four for B.S.W.s). These credentials are particularly valuable for social workers in private practice, as some health insurance providers require them for reimbursement purposes. Contact the association for more information.

### Other Requirements

Social work requires great dedication. As a social worker, you have the responsibility of helping whole families, groups, and communities, as well as focusing on the needs of individuals. Your efforts will not always be supported by society at large; sometimes you must work against a community's prejudice, disinterest, and denial. You must also remain sensitive to the problems of your clients, offering support rather than moral judgment or personal bias. The only way to effectively address new social problems and new client groups is to remain open to the thoughts and needs of all human beings. Assessing situations and solving problems requires clarity of vision and a genuine concern for the well-being of others.

With this clarity of vision, your work will be all the more rewarding. Social workers have the satisfaction of making a connection with other people and helping them through difficult times. Along with the rewards, however, the work can cause a great deal of stress. Hearing repeatedly about the deeply troubled lives of prison inmates, the mentally ill, abused women and children, and others can be depressing and defeating. Trying to convince society of the need for changes in laws and services can be a long, hard struggle. You must have perseverance to fight for your clients against all odds.

## EXPLORING

Ask a counselor or teacher to arrange an information interview with a social worker. Read books and magazines about social work.

As a high school student, you may find openings for summer or part-time work as a receptionist or file clerk with a local social service agency. If there are no opportunities for paid employment, you could work as a volunteer. You can also gain good experience by working as a counselor in a camp for children with physical, mental, or developmental disabilities. Your local YMCA, park district, or other recreational facility may need volunteers for group recreation programs, including programs designed for the prevention of delinquency. By reporting for your high school newspaper, you'll have the opportunity to interview people, conduct surveys, and research social change, all of which are important aspects of the social work profession.

You could also volunteer a few afternoons a week to read to people in retirement homes or to the blind. Work as a tutor in special education programs is sometimes available to high school students.

## EMPLOYERS

Approximately 642,000 social workers are employed in the United States. About 46 percent of this number are child, family, and school social workers. Twenty-two percent work in medical and public health, and 21 percent work in mental health and substance abuse social work. Social workers can be employed in direct or clinical practice, providing individual and family counseling services, or they may work as administrators for the organizations that provide direct practice. Social workers are employed by community health and mental health centers; general and psychiatric hospitals; child care, family services, and community service organizations, including day care and Head Start programs; elderly care programs, including adult protective services and adult day care and foster care; prisons; shelters and halfway houses; schools; courts; and nursing homes.

## STARTING OUT

Most students of social work pursue a master's degree and in the process learn about the variety of jobs available. They also make valuable connections through faculty and other students. Through the university's career services office or an internship program, a student will learn about job openings and potential employers.

A social work education in an accredited program will provide you with the most opportunities, and the best salaries and chances for promotion, but practical social work experience can also earn you full-time employment. A part-time job or volunteer work will introduce you to social work professionals who can provide you with career guidance and letters of reference. Agencies with limited funding may not be able to afford to hire social workers with M.S.W.s and therefore will look for applicants with a great deal of experience and lower salary expectations.

## ADVANCEMENT

More attractive and better-paying jobs tend to go to those with more years of practical experience. Dedication to your job, an extensive resume, and good references will lead to advancement in the profession. Also, many social work programs offer continuing education workshops, courses, and seminars. These refresher courses help practicing social workers to refine their skills and to learn about new areas of practice and new methods and problems. The courses are intended to supplement your social work education, not substitute for a bachelor's or master's degree. These continuing education courses can lead to job promotions and salary increases.

## EARNINGS

The more education a social worker has completed, the more money he or she stands to make in the profession. The area of practice also determines earnings; the areas of mental health, group services, and community organization and planning provide higher salaries, while elderly and disabled care generally provide lower pay.

The median salary for child, family, and school social workers was $39,960 in 2009, according to the U.S. Department of Labor. The top paid 10 percent earned more than $67,360, while the lowest paid 10 percent earned less than $26,050. Medical and public health social workers' salaries ranged from less than $28,600 to more than $71,190 with a median salary of $46,300 in 2009, and mental health and substance abuse workers earned between $24,940 and $62,760 with a median salary of $38,200.

Most full-time positions provide life and medical insurance, pension plans, and paid vacation and holidays.

## WORK ENVIRONMENT

Social workers do not always work at a desk. When they do, they may be interviewing clients, writing reports, or conferring with other staff members. Depending on the size of the agency, office duties such as typing letters, filing, and answering phones may be performed by an aide or volunteer. Social workers employed at shelters or halfway houses may spend most of their time with clients, tutoring, counseling, or leading groups.

Some social workers have to drive to remote areas to make a home visit. They may go into inner-city neighborhoods, schools, courts, or jails. In larger cities, domestic violence and homeless shelters are sometimes located in rundown or dangerous areas. Most social workers are involved directly with the people they serve and must carefully examine the client's living conditions and family relations. Although some of these living conditions can be pleasant and demonstrate a good home situation, others can be squalid and depressing.

Advocacy involves work in a variety of different environments. Although much of this work may require making phone calls and sending e-mails, faxes, and letters, it also requires meetings with clients' employers, directors of agencies, local legislators, and others. It may sometimes require testifying in court as well.

## OUTLOOK

The field of social work is expected to grow faster than the average for all occupations through 2018, according to the U.S. Department of Labor. The greatest factor for this growth is the increased number of older people who are in need of social services. Social workers who specialize in gerontology will find many job opportunities in assisted-living and senior-living communities, nursing homes, hospitals, long-term care facilities, hospices, and home health care agencies. The needs of the future elderly population are likely to be different from those of the present elderly. Currently, the elderly appreciate community living, while subsequent generations may demand more individual care. Employment in medical and public health social work is expected to grow by 22 percent by 2018—or much faster than the average for all careers.

Schools will also need more social workers to deal with issues such as teenage pregnancies, children from single-parent households, and any adjustment problems recent immigrants may have. The trend to integrate students with disabilities into the general school population will require the expertise of social workers to make the transition smoother. However, job availability in schools will depend on funding given by state and local sources.

To help control costs, hospitals are encouraging early discharge for some of their patients. Social workers will be needed by hospitals to help secure health services for patients in their homes. There is also a growing number of people with physical disabilities or impairments staying in their own homes, requiring home health care workers. Opportunities for social workers in nursing homes, long-term care facilities, and hospices should also increase.

Employment for mental health and substance abuse social workers is expected to grow by 20 percent by 2018; it is the second fastest growing subspecialty in the field. The field of substance abuse social work should be especially strong as courts increasingly place substance abusers in treatment programs instead of prison or as a condition of their sentencing or probation.

Increased availability of health insurance funding and the growing number of people able to pay for professional help will create opportunities for those in private practice. Many businesses hire social workers to help in employee assistance programs, often on a contractual basis.

Poverty is still a main issue that social workers address. Families are finding it increasingly challenging to make ends meet on wages that are just barely above the minimum. The problem of fathers who do not make their court-ordered child support payments forces single mothers to work more than one job or rely on welfare. An increased awareness of domestic violence has also focused attention on the fact that many homeless and unemployed people are women who have left abusive situations. Besides all this, working with the poor is often considered unattractive, leaving many social work positions in this area unfilled.

Competition for jobs in urban areas will remain strong. However, there is still a shortage of social workers in rural areas; these areas usually cannot offer the high salaries or modern facilities that attract large numbers of applicants.

The social work profession is constantly changing. The survival of social service agencies, both private and public, depends on shifting political, economic, and workplace issues.

Social work professionals are worried about the threat of declining professional standards. Because of budget constraints and a need for more workers, some agencies have lowered their job requirements. When unable to afford qualified professionals, they hire those with less education and experience. This downgrading raises questions about quality of care and professional standards. Just as in some situations low salaries push out the qualified social worker, so do high salaries. In the area of corrections, attractive salaries (up to $40,000 for someone with a two-year associate's degree) have resulted in more competition from other service workers.

Liability is another growing concern. If a social worker, for example, tries to prove that a child has been beaten or attempts to remove a child from his or her home, the worker can potentially be sued for libel. At the other extreme, a social worker can face criminal charges for failure to remove a child from an abusive home. More social workers are taking out malpractice insurance.

## FOR MORE INFORMATION

*To read articles about geriatric care-related issues, visit the association's Web site.*
Association for Gerontology Education in Social Work
http://www.agesocialwork.org

*For information on licensing, contact*
Association of Social Work Boards
400 South Ridge Parkway, Suite B
Culpeper, VA 22701-3791
Tel: 800-225-6880
http://www.aswb.org

*For information on social work careers and educational programs, contact*
Council on Social Work Education
1701 Duke Street, Suite 200
Alexandria, VA 22314-3457
Tel: 703-683-8080
E-mail: info@cswe.org
http://www.cswe.org

*To access the online publication* Choices: Careers in Social Work, *contact*
National Association of Social Workers
750 First Street, NE, Suite 700
Washington, DC 20002-4241
Tel: 202-408-8600

E-mail: membership@naswdc.org
http://www.naswdc.org

*For information on educational programs in Canada, contact*
**Canadian Association of Schools of Social Work**
1398 Star Top Road
Ottawa, ON K1B 4V7 Canada
Tel: 613-792-1953
E-mail: cassw@cassw-acess.ca
http://www.cassw-acess.ca

*For career information and job listings available in Canada, contact*
**Canadian Association of Social Workers**
383 Parkdale Avenue, Suite 402
Ottawa, ON K1Y 4R4 Canada
Tel: 613-729-6668
E-mail: casw@casw-acts.ca
http://www.casw-acts.ca

## ═══ INTERVIEW ═══

*Christine Hains is a social worker and the foster care program supervisor for an adoption and orphan care nonprofit agency in Michigan. She discussed her career with the editors of* Careers in Focus: Social Work.

**Q. What made you want to become a social worker?**
**A.** When I was in high school I took a class that addressed child abuse and neglect. I felt the importance of these two social work roles and felt drawn toward this field through these two tracks.

**Q. What is one thing that young people may not know about a career in social work?**
**A.** It can take a lot of time and energy. There is a lot of paperwork to do and regulations to follow and in the field I am in workers do not get as much client contact as they would think. Other areas of social work may get more, but there are a lot of other duties on top of the client contact.

**Q. What are typical duties for foster care workers?**
**A.** Foster care workers carry a caseload of cases in which the children are temporary or permanent wards of the court.

They work with the birth families (when overseeing temporary wards) and work together on a plan for the family to work on reunification. The worker writes reports, is the contact person for services, and documents the progress in the other services the parents are involved in. They testify in court regarding the progress the family has made or not made and makes recommendations based on service provider reports and their input on progress regarding progress towards reunification. During a typical day, they may conduct home visits, make phone calls, write reports, fill out paperwork for referrals, talk with service providers regarding progress, handle crisis situations, observe parenting time between birth parents and children, and work with the foster parents to ensure the children are getting the services and care they need. They are the primary worker on a case and are in charge of making sure the families are complying with court orders and treatment plans.

Q. **What are some of the pros and cons of your job?**
A. Pros: Being able to provide resources and services for low-income, substance- and mental health-affected parents who don't know how to advocate or get the assistance they need. Meeting really neat children who have been through great trauma and seeing how they can flourish in the right environment. The flexibility of the job is also an advantage.

Cons: Very busy work (sometimes you have to work overtime), stressful situations when parents and others can be upset with decisions the worker has to make, and policy requirements that are oftentimes hard to meet.

Q. **What are the most important personal and professional qualities for people in your career?**
A. You need to be a strong advocate, able to handle crisis and conflict situations, have the ability to speak up and be strong in decision making, and have good time management, organizational, and interpersonal skills.

Q. **What activities would you suggest to high school students who are interested in this career?**
A. Shadow workers in court, interview workers in the area they are interested to see how the "real job" may differ from their thoughts about the positions, and volunteer at agencies in their areas of interest.

**Q. What advice would you give to young people who are interested in the field?**

**A.** Make sure you speak with others in the field and volunteer so you can get a good feel for your area of interest. Be prepared to do much more paperwork than you may think. You need to be able to make decisions and handle crisis situations.

# Index

Entries and page numbers in **bold** indicate major treatment of a topic.

## A